CONTENTS

About This Publication. Since 1980, *New Directions for Teaching and Learning (NDTL)* has brought a unique blend of theory, research, and practice to leaders in postsecondary education. *NDTL* sourcebooks strive not only for solid substance but also for timeliness, compactness, and accessibility.

The series has four goals: to inform readers about current and future directions in teaching and learning in postsecondary education, to illuminate the context that shapes these new directions, to illustrate these new directions through examples from real settings, and to propose ways in which these new directions can be incorporated into still other settings.

This publication reflects our view that teaching deserves respect as a high form of scholarship. We believe that significant scholarship is conducted not only by researchers who report results of empirical investigations but also by practitioners who share disciplined reflections about teaching. Contributors to *NDTL* approach questions of teaching and learning as seriously as they approach substantive questions in their own disciplines, and they deal not only with pedagogical issues but also with the intellectual and social context in which these issues arise. Authors deal on the one hand with theory and research and on the other with practice, and they translate from research and theory to practice and back again.

About This Volume. Eleanor Willemsen and Joanne Gainen address the problems that students experience in courses that serve as "gateways" to several majors. Most of these gateway courses have been stumbling blocks for many students, resulting in a narrowing of the student population in those disciplines. This volume asks what instructors can do to help those students succeed instead.

Robert J. Menges, *Editor-in-Chief*
Marilla D. Svinicki, *Associate Editor*

ROBERT J. MENGES, editor-in-chief, is professor of education and social policy at Northwestern University, and senior researcher, National Center on Post-secondary Teaching, Learning, and Assessment.

MARILLA D. SVINICKI, associate editor, is director of the Center for Teaching Effectiveness, University of Texas at Austin.

EDITORS' NOTES

Aspiring scientists and professionals begin their educations in a small subset of challenging, sequentially organized, quantitatively oriented courses. For the sciences and engineering, the courses include physics, chemistry, biology, and calculus. Students entering business majors take accounting, economics, and statistics. In social sciences like psychology and sociology, too, majors in the first year or two are usually required to take courses in statistics and research methods.

Courses such as these can open the gates or block the way for students interested in scientific, technical, and professional careers. Because such careers are potentially interesting and rewarding, women and students of color increasingly choose science, mathematics, engineering (SME) majors (Hilton and Lee, 1988). The problem remains, however, that students are also switching out of these majors in disproportionately high numbers. For example, although about 50 percent of students persist in their original major in both SME and humanities/social sciences (Hum/SS), a total of 74 percent remain within Hum/SS compared with just 56 percent in SME majors (Seymour and Hewitt, 1994, p. 37; excludes computer science). Patterns differ for men and women: although about half of men remain in their original SME major, and approximately 60 percent remain in the SME group, only 48 percent of women remain in SME majors. Persistence is lowest for mathematics/statistics and computer science (approximately 30 percent remain in each) compared with 65 percent remaining within the humanities/social science cluster. Men shift to humanities and fine arts (33 percent), business (26 percent), and computer science (21 percent). Women shift primarily to humanities and fine arts (51 percent) and education (21 percent), consistent with conservative cultural expectations for women (Seymour and Hewitt, 1994, pp. 35–45). Many students who remain in SME majors express dissatisfaction on a variety of dimensions.

The crucial experiences affecting students' decision to persist in or switch out of quantitative majors often occur during the first year of study at the college level, when they must successfully complete challenging "gateway" courses required. As reported in Chapter One of this volume, an estimated 35 percent of students who choose SME majors abandon their plans between the freshman and sophomore years; freshman-sophomore attrition estimates for students of color range from 50 percent to 65 percent.

Conflicting cultural assumptions and values may underlie much of the discontent that causes students to leave quantitative majors. The classroom culture in quantitatively oriented courses may be comfortable for or at least familiar to some students but antithetical to the assumptions and values that other students bring with them. For example, students who are involved in competitive sports may expect and even welcome competition in the classroom environment. In contrast, students whose cultural values place concern for the well-being of the community above individual achievement may experience alienation when professors reward only competitive, individualistic efforts. Similarly, students socialized to value teacher authority and "objective" knowledge (portrayed in psychological literature as "dualistic" thinking or "received knowledge"; Perry, 1970; Belenky, Clinchy, Goldberger, and Tarule, 1986) may find lecture-oriented courses with cookbook labs unsurprising, while students who value "subjective" or "constructed" knowledge (Belenky, Clinchy, Goldberger, and Tarule, 1986) find learning more rewarding when they are able to participate in making sense of concepts and ideas in the classroom and laboratory (see chapters Five and Seven). When the conflict in values, assumptions, and expectations is too great, anxiety rises to the point where it blocks learning, students begin to feel "I can't do math" and "I prefer to learn where I feel more welcome and valued and can enjoy what I am learning."

This volume shows how the teaching and learning culture in quantitatively oriented courses can be changed—not by sacrificing standards and principles of objectivity but by opening the gates to active, collaborative student participation in the construction of knowledge using the methods and tools of the quantitative disciplines and professions. The first two chapters frame the problem. In Chapter One, Gainen presents data on students' persistence in quantitatively oriented majors and analyzes the role of cultural and other influences on their success in these majors. In Chapter Two, Willemsen frames the problem in psychological terms: students who acquire a sense of "I can't do it!" in quantitative courses early in their college careers are unlikely to feel welcome or capable in the majors these courses support.

Chapter Three is a pivotal one for our argument that the culture in quantitative courses can be changed without sacrificing quality. Bonsangue and Drew report results of a longitudinal study of the calculus workshop approach. Their findings demonstrate that challenging (as opposed to remedial) instructional experiences for women and students of color dramatically increase their success in quantitative courses and their subsequent persistence in SME majors.

Chapters Four through Nine show the reader how quantitative gateway courses can be changed to involve students more deeply and facilitate their learning. In Chapter Four, Ditzler and Ricci illustrate how chemistry is more inviting to students when they are involved in the discovery processes of the discipline. Chapter Five, by Pavelich, Olds, and Miller, takes the inquiry process into the field. Students in their freshman-sophomore engineering sequence interact with actual clients to develop and present solutions to real-world problems. Students in Troeger's introductory computer science class, in Chapter Six, learn to tackle significant programming problems using logic and preparatory design work in a collaborative context guided by peer facilitators. Chapter Seven, by Sanchez, Hight, and Gainen, is a case study of how a model of intellectual development influenced the evolution of an introductory engineering graphics course. In Chapter Eight, Laws, Rosborough, and Poodry describe results of the highly successful workshop physics program—and report some counterintuitive findings regarding women's responses to the active learning pedagogy of the course. Concluding the set, in Chapter Nine Pincus describes a comprehensive reform project in accounting that integrates the introductory sequence and incorporates active learning throughout.

Can these authors' innovations be adapted to other disciplines? Chapter Ten tests the portability of the models by applying lessons learned in the rest of the book to the redesign of Willemsen's introductory statistics course, which is first described in Chapter Two. We identify seven pedagogical characteristics of the innovative courses described in this collection and then incorporate them within a larger framework, the "cognitive apprenticeship" model of Collins, Brown, and Newman (1989).

We hope that the descriptions of the programs, the data that support their effectiveness, and our attempt to reenvision statistics will encourage readers to apply these concepts in their own courses so that more students can pass through the gateway and pursue the challenging and rewarding careers they seek.

References

Belenky, M., Clinchy, B. M., Goldberger, N., and Tarule, J. *Women's Ways of Knowing: The Development of Self, Voice, and Mind.* New York: Basic Books, 1986.

Collins, A., Brown, J. S., and Newman, S. E. "Cognitive Apprenticeship: Teaching the Craft of Reading, Writing, and Mathematics." In L. B. Resnick (ed.), *Knowing, Learning, and Instruction: Essays in Honor of Robert Glaser.* Hillsdale, N.J.: Erlbaum, 1989.

Hilton, T. L., and Lee, V. E. "Student Interest and Persistence in Science: Changes in the Educational Pipeline in the Last Decade." *Journal of Higher Education,* 1988, *59* (5), 510–526.

Perry, W. G., Jr. *Forms of Intellectual and Ethical Development in the College Years: A Scheme.* Troy, Mo.: Holt, Rinehart & Winston, 1970.

Seymour, E., and Hewitt, N. M. *Talking About Leaving: Factors Contributing to High Attrition Rates Among Science, Mathematics, and Engineering Undergraduate Majors.* Final report to the Alfred P. Sloan Foundation on an ethnographic inquiry at seven institutions. Boulder: University of Colorado Bureau of Sociological Research, 1994.

Joanne Gainen
Eleanor W. Willemsen
Editors

JOANNE GAINEN is director of the Teaching and Learning Center at Santa Clara University, where she works with faculty to foster active learning, critical thinking, and a supportive learning environment in courses for an increasingly diverse student population. She is the author of Critical Thinking: Theory, Research, Practice, and Possibilities *(ASHE-ERIC, 1988) and coeditor (with R. Boice) of* Building a Diverse Faculty, New Directions for Teaching and Learning, *no. 53.*

ELEANOR W. WILLEMSEN is professor of psychology at Santa Clara University, where she uses active learning methods to teach statistics and developmental psychology. She also serves as an advocate for children in the foster care system.

Faculty may be able to reduce student attrition from quantitative majors by addressing four barriers to success—precollege preparation, peer culture, classroom climate, and instructional style—in introductory courses in these fields.

Barriers to Success in Quantitative Gatekeeper Courses

Joanne Gainen

Success for students in introductory courses at the gateway to science, math, and business majors courses—whether calculus, chemistry, or accounting—does not come easily. Students frequently fail to complete these courses satisfactorily on the first attempt. Negatively skewed grade distributions are considered a fact of life. Thus it is not surprising that the greatest attrition among students interested in majoring in science, mathematics, and engineering (SME) occurs between the freshman and sophomore years. An estimated 35 percent of students who choose SME majors when they enter college switch out of them or leave college altogether between the freshman and sophomore years; among students of color, attrition is much higher (National Academy of Sciences, 1987; Seymour and Hewitt, 1994). Similarly, the introductory accounting sequence challenges many would-be business majors, with attrition disproportionately high among African American males (Carpenter, Friar, and Lipe, 1993).

Many educators feel that poor performance and high attrition in quantitative majors and courses are regrettable but not surprising. Not everyone has the aptitude or the motivation to succeed in these challenging courses, the argument goes, and the students are better off discovering their limitations early on. Today, however, the conventional wisdom—that students who leave or avoid quantitative fields of study are ill-prepared or simply "not cut out for" mathematics-based careers—is being challenged. Students who choose such majors are generally well prepared in mathematics and science (Rawls, 1991; Widnall, 1988). Close to half report GPAs of A– or better, whereas only about one-fourth of students selecting other majors do (Green, 1989).

Why does the U.S. educational system lose so many potential scientists, mathematicians, and engineers? This chapter examines why some students succeed while others, with comparable ability and interest, decide, "I can't— or won't—do it." Four factors are explored: college preparation; peer culture; the classroom climate; and the competitive, impersonal culture of many of these courses.

College Preparation

The precollege educational experiences of many young people severely limit their access to the knowledge, problem-solving skills, and academic orientation necessary to succeed in quantitative majors. The most dramatic and frequent limiting factor is insufficient or inadequate preparation in mathematics. Mathematics ability is a strong predictor of success in engineering (Levin and Wyckoff, 1988) and is highly correlated with GPA in accounting (Herring and Izard, 1992). But by ninth grade, only about half of all students are likely to have a sufficient mathematics background to remain on the path to quantitative careers. Among high school graduates, only about one-fourth have sufficient mathematics and science preparation to move directly into SME majors in college (Office of Technology Assessment, 1985; cited in Widnall, 1988, pp. 29–30). Women are especially disadvantaged at the high school level. Only 11 percent of women, compared with 14 percent of men, have an adequate mathematics background upon completing high school (Office of Technology Assessment, 1985). Among high school graduates in 1987, 25 percent of men had credits in physics, compared with 15 percent of women; approximately 8 percent of men had calculus credits, compared with 5 percent of women (Westat, Inc., 1987; cited in Brush, 1991, p. 408).

For African Americans, Latinos, and Native Americans, problems of access are compounded by the poor quality of precollege education. Schools dominated by students of color have far more limited mathematics and science curricula than schools with predominantly white student populations; for example, only half of secondary schools with minority enrollments of at least 90 percent offer calculus whereas four-fifths of schools with white enrollments of 90 percent or higher do. In poor, inner-city schools where students of color are in the majority, teachers are less qualified and less well paid than teachers in predominantly white schools and many teach subjects outside their area of certification. Students of color are more likely than their white counterparts to be assigned to classes with poorly trained teachers within a given school (Oakes, 1990).

Countering Limited Preparation. Recognizing the inequities in college preparation, federal agencies have developed programs to interest young people, particularly students of color, in science and mathematics. Funding is channeled through programs such as the Young Scholars Program Early Alert Initiative and Summer Science Camps (NSF); Minority Science Improvement

Program (MISP; Department of Education); Energy Prefreshman Enrichment Program (PREP; Department of Energy); and NASA's Education Program (Witter, 1993).

Until the long-term benefits of these programs take effect, more immediate measures are needed to help students compensate for gaps in their precollege educations. One strategy is to offer summer transition programs for students about to enter college. For example, at Xavier University, a historically black institution in New Orleans, the Stress on Analytical Reasoning program (SOAR) has for many years fostered success of students interested in medicine and other science-related careers (Carmichael and Sevenair, 1991). The new CHALLENGE transition program, at Georgia Institute of Technology, is a four-week "academic preseason" designed to help students of color succeed in technical fields. Students learn calculus, chemistry, psychology, and computer skills; psychology is given for credit to reduce time pressure in the crucial first quarter. Students also learn time management and planning skills. First-quarter GPAs for the 1991–92 cohort averaged 2.6 compared with an average of 2.2 for similar students in past years; in the second year, after implementing improvements based on Total Quality Management, GPAs averaged 3.3 (Seymour, 1993).

Peer Culture

Poor college preparation helps explain the limitations of some students but it does not account for attrition among those who have the necessary interest and skills and yet fail to pursue quantitative majors. Once students enter college, the peer culture can influence the direction and intensity of their efforts. For example, a major predictor of individual students' self-reported orientation to academics is the percentage of students in the institution as a whole who describe themselves as academically oriented (Astin, 1993). The peer culture of an institution may be especially important in influencing women to pursue advanced degrees: women are more likely to pursue the doctorate in any field (including the sciences) if they graduate from an institution with large numbers of women who are serious about academics, regardless of their particular fields of study (Tidball and Kistiakowsky, 1976).

When peers are negative toward or uninterested in academics, students may find it difficult to maintain momentum in the face of the academic challenges of SME and other majors with a strong quantitative component. In contrast, when students are affiliated with a peer culture that favors academic pursuits, they are much more likely to succeed in these challenging majors. Two studies illustrate the influence of peers on persistence in SME majors, one the negative influence, the other the positive.

Culture of Romance. A peer culture focused on relationships rather than academics may diminish some women's aspirations (Holland and Eisenhart, 1990). A study at two southern women's colleges (one historically black) of twenty-three women found that peer ties—and particularly romantic relation-ships—took precedence over academics for all but about one-fourth of the sample. The women in the study had strong academic records and career aspi-rations. About half planned to pursue majors in math or science. Yet in their first three semesters on campus, the majority quickly adapted to a peer culture in which attractiveness to men was "a major route to self-worth and prestige" (p. 118), and in which being known for academic achievements could be detrimental to social standing. In particular, students interested in math and science—whether male or female—were considered "weird" by their peers (pp. 164–165).

The "culture of romance" did not influence all women equally. *Credential-oriented women,* who viewed education solely as a means to earn job-related credentials, treated academic requirements as obstacles to be overcome rather than as preparation for future careers. They avoided academic challenges and often failed to complete their intended degrees. *Approval-oriented women,* who had usually done well in high school with little effort, questioned their "natural abilities" and scaled down their aspirations (primarily in the sciences) on find-ing that good grades in college required more effort than they expected. Only six women, whose idea of education was to learn from experts, maintained or intensified their academic aspirations. As college undergraduates, they sought challenging learning experiences and viewed grades as indicators of learning and development. They limited their romantic relationships and balanced aca-demic and social interests. Four years after college, only the members of this group were found to have gone on to graduate school. In contrast, the women who focused on obtaining credentials or approval found themselves in careers that lacked financial and intellectual rewards and in traditional female roles, in spite of their innate abilities and aspirations. Because of a peer culture that portrayed romance and education as competing interests, these women had failed to develop a self-image based on career success (p. 184).

Peer Group Interaction. When the peer culture does not support aca-demic work, isolating oneself may appear to be a reasonable response. How-ever, research on African American and Chinese American students taking mathematics courses at the University of California at Berkeley revealed the risks of such a choice. Treisman (1985) found that African American students at Berkeley maintained a distinct separation between academic work and social life yet still did poorly in calculus. Only two out of the twenty-one African American students enrolled in elementary calculus in 1975 completed the three-course sequence with a grade of C or better. Between 1973 and 1976, sophomore-level calculus was completed with a C or better by only four out of forty African Americans. In contrast, Chinese American students were frequently among the strongest students in these courses. In search of an expla-nation, Treisman found striking differences between the practices of the African American and Chinese American students.

• Chinese American students studied in groups; African Americans studied alone.

- In their groups, Chinese American students helped each other with home-work problems and exchanged information about academic life.
- Chinese American students spent about fourteen hours a week doing school-work, including about two hours of individual study per each hour of group study. African American students studied about eight hours per week—the traditionally prescribed two hours per class hour.
- Chinese American students helped each other determine when their diffi-culty on a particular problem was just computational and could be solved by themselves and when they needed help from a TA. African Americans rarely sought help from peers or TAs and did not use the tutoring services available on campus. Instead, they spent much time in frustrating searches for a solution when their results did not match those given in the back of the book.
- Chinese American students engaged in "friendly competition" for the fastest or best solution to a problem but shared essential knowledge to benefit the entire group.

In short, Chinese American students used the peer group as a resource for learning; African American students did not.

Redirecting Peer Energies. Although it may be difficult to influence a strongly entrenched peer culture like the culture of romance described earlier, it is possible to provide significant alternatives by arranging academic experi-ences to capitalize on the importance of peer relationships. This principle guided the design of what is now called the Emerging Scholars Program (ESP) at Berkeley. In addition to attending class regularly, students meet in small groups for several hours each week to work on challenging problems guided by an undergraduate facilitator. Focusing on academic excellence rather than remediation, these programs teach students to work constructively with peers to develop the knowledge, skills, and motivation that will enable them to suc-ceed. The workshops dramatically increased the success of African American students in Treisman's study (1985). A similar program made up primarily of Latinos increased their persistence in SME majors to a rate nearly double that of their nonworkshop peers. For women, the success rate was even more dramatic—100 percent versus 52 percent completion rates for their nonwork-shop peers (Bonsangue and Drew, 1992; and Chapter Three of this volume).

These and other successes with peer-facilitated programs (such as sup-plemental instruction described by Blanc, DeBuhr, and Martin, 1983) demon-strate that the potentially negative influence of the peer culture can be transformed into a powerful positive force for learning and long-term academic success.

Classroom Climate

Within the classroom itself, a "chilly climate" can deter women and students of color by making them feel uncomfortable and out of place (Hall and Sandler, 1982). Climate issues for both women and students of color are especially salient in quantitative fields, where such students are relative new-comers (Brush, 1991; Seymour and Hewitt, 1994).

The chilly climate may be subtle, taking the form of male domination of classroom discussions, for example. In one study of classes taught by male teachers, male students spoke longer than women (Krupnick, 1984). Women spoke in brief episodes of a few seconds and were more frequently interrupted; once interrupted, they tended not to speak again during that class period. Once men started talking, they talked for longer periods without interruption. Women in classrooms dominated by men in this way have less opportunity to experience the benefits of participation, including enhancement of learning and critical thinking skills, and opportunities to gain recognition for their ideas.

Students of color too are likely to find that their opportunities to con-tribute to and benefit from class discussion are limited. An observational study of sixteen college classrooms taught by white males and enrolling at least two black students revealed three significant differences between these professors' responses to minority and nonminority students. Even though minority stu-dents initiated as many contacts as nonminority students, professors addressed more high-level questions to nonminority students, more often helped non-minority students to clarify their answers, and spent more time responding to the questions of nonminority students (with type of question statistically held constant). These professors also acknowledged having lower expectations for minority students (Trujillo, 1986). Students in such classrooms may find them-selves ill at ease yet unable to pinpoint the source of their discomfort. The cumulative impact, however, is likely to be a feeling that they are not welcome in the classroom or the discipline.

In addition to these relatively subtle forms of exclusion, women and students of color report many experiences of overt sexism or racism. For exam-ple, faculty may express concern about their ability to handle the stress of highly competitive, technical courses, suggesting that they question the stu-dents' abilities and the appropriateness of their participation in SME disci-plines. Women report that they encounter "daily irritation caused by sexist remarks from male peers" (Seymour, 1992, p. 289; Seymour and Hewitt, 1994). Male classmates often fail to treat them as intellectual equals, instead downplaying their academic success or responding to them primarily in sex-ual terms—behavior that is often overlooked by male professors. This kind of behavior forces women to choose between concealing their femininity or feel-ing like outsiders in a male culture (Seymour and Hewitt, 1994). Women in the calculus workshop program, discussed in Chapter Three, who all persisted in SME majors, reported "barriers of sexism" within their majors, contributing to feelings of isolation and self-doubt (Bonsangue and Drew, 1992, p. 19). Such experiences may help to account for the decline in women's self-esteem during college, even among those who are class valedictorians and whose GPAs are higher than their male counterparts (Arnold, 1987).

Teachers may unintentionally convey lesser expectations for women and students of color because they do not fit preconceived notions of scientists, engineers, mathematicians, or other quantitatively oriented professionals or academics. For example, the invisibility of women in SME textbooks, portrayals of students in SME majors as "nerds," and perceptions of SME fields as "unfeminine" all contribute to a climate that is particularly difficult for women in these technical fields (Brush, 1991; Seymour and Hewitt, 1994). Students of color feel most exposed and vulnerable when they are a small minority, even though, paradoxically, white students express greater hostility on campuses with larger proportions of students of color. In these circumstances minority students often band together and personally experience less overt racism (Seymour and Hewitt, 1994).

Improving the Classroom Climate. Awareness of climate issues by faculty is essential to counteract both subtle and overt messages suggesting to women and students of color that they have little to contribute to the course or the discipline. Training programs in which class discussions are videotaped and analyzed in a supportive setting can help faculty recognize patterns and redirect classroom conversations so that opportunities to participate are more equitably distributed. Ground rules for group interactions, developed by students in the class, can also help to counteract imbalances in class discussions and laboratory work and to foster a respectful, inclusive classroom climate. Instructors can also survey their classes periodically for feedback on climate issues and then discuss results with the class to communicate expectations of inclusive behavior.

Course Culture

Many students learn best in a context that invites personal connection to professors, peers, and the subject matter. For these students, the impersonal, competitive culture often found in gatekeeper courses conflicts with their values and expectations. For example, some SME programs actively discourage students in order to "weed out" all but the most talented and dedicated (Seymour and Hewitt, 1994), resulting in a competitive ethos that is rejected by many students, particularly women (Brush, 1991). Moreover, introductory SME courses are simply unstimulating for a significant number of well-qualified students (Seymour and Hewitt, 1994). Similarly, in accounting, traditional introductory lecture courses convey an image of the profession that is more impersonal and rule-governed than is true in practice, thus discouraging—or failing to attract—students with the more conceptual learning style needed for success in the accounting profession today (Wyer, 1993; Pincus, Chapter Nine, this volume).

The role of instructional culture in student attrition emerges clearly in a multi-institution interview study of 335 capable students (with quantitative SAT scores of 650 or above) who either persisted in or switched out of SME majors. About 75 percent of all interviewees (including both switchers and nonswitchers) and 89 percent of those who switched complained of "bad teaching" in science courses. Bad teaching was described to include lecturing rather than explaining, illustrating, applying, or discussing; not being able to or refusing to explain difficult ideas; reading from texts rather than explaining; doing 'silent teaching' (writing on the blackboard rather than explaining material); emphasizing testing and rote learning rather than comprehension; not offering intellectual stimulation, challenge, or encouragement to think critically; failing to teach for knowledge transfer; offering dull material and presentation; failing to communicate enthusiasm for the subject; being inflexible or defensive in response to questions and discussion points; and having an unapproachable demeanor (Seymour, 1992, p. 286).

Both switchers and nonswitchers also objected to the fast-paced, overloaded curriculum, and roughly half of both groups cited poor advising and unhelpful faculty as problems (Seymour, 1992). The instructional environment these students describe suggests that SME disciplines value impersonal objectivity, involve isolated individual effort, and require innate ability. The message many students hear is something like this: "Science is a matter of fact (or mathematics is a matter of reasoning); there is nothing to discuss. If you can't figure it out on your own you probably won't make it in this field anyway, so you might as well give up now."

In Seymour and Hewitt's study, many women and minorities who were "turned on" to science and mathematics by caring high school teachers were "turned off" by the impersonal culture they encountered in SME courses in college. Confronted with a culture they found hostile and alienating, students reported "weighing the profit-to-grief ratio." Finding their current academic work unsatisfying, they looked for an eventual payoff in material rewards and career opportunities. Many found the ratio too low: lack of material rewards was cited as a causal factor for their switch by about 40 percent of women switchers (Seymour and Hewitt, 1994), and two-thirds of them cited rejection of the "lifestyle" associated with the field (Seymour, 1992). Thus for a large pool of students with an interest in and aptitude for scientific and mathematical work, the instructional culture in gateway courses and in SME majors in general was a significant deterrent to persistence.

Changing the Instructional Culture. Many institutions have worked hard to recruit students of color, and these students, along with women, are increasingly choosing SME majors upon entering college (Hilton and Lee, 1988). The logical next step for the receiving departments is to sustain their interest and develop their talents. In addition, students who do not plan to major in quantitative subjects should have the opportunity to acquire competence in and develop appreciation for scientific and mathematical inquiry.

The success of these students depends at least in part on the willingness of faculty to resist the cultural norms of competition and "received knowledge" and the impersonality associated with introductory quantitative courses. Departmental commitment to helping students succeed in the all-important introductory sequence is an essential first step—not by diluting course content or lowering standards but by showing students what it was that attracted faculty themselves to these subjects. The very best teachers should be assigned to these courses and given ample assistance to teach well. Class sizes should be limited to facilitate discussion; where this is not feasible, faculty can organize peer-facilitated discussion sections, study groups, or academic excellence workshops (Bonsangue and Drew, this volume; Treisman, 1985) to create a more stimulating and welcoming environment for all students. The remaining chapters in this volume illustrate faculty efforts to implement a new kind of instructional culture in courses at the gateway to quantitative majors.

Conclusion

One final point deserves attention. Programs that successfully attract and retain students in quantitative majors bear the imprint of faculty collaboration. When faculty work together to improve students' learning, the stage is set for a more cooperative and less fragmented departmental culture. Faculty discover new challenges and intellectual engagement in the common enterprise of sharing their discipline with a new generation of learners who, although different from themselves, are fully capable of succeeding in—and enjoying—quantitative gateway courses.

References

Arnold, K. "Retaining High-Achieving Women in Science and Engineering." Paper presented at the AAS Symposium on Women and Girls in Science and Technology, University of Michigan, Ann Arbor, July 1987.

Astin, A. *What Matters in College? Four Critical Years Revisited.* San Francisco: Jossey-Bass, 1993.

Blanc, R. A., DeBuhr, L. E., and Martin, D. C. "Breaking the Attrition Cycle: The Effects of Supplemental Instruction on Undergraduate Performance and Attrition." *Journal of Higher Education,* 1983, 54 (1), 80–90.

Bonsangue, M. V., and Drew, D. E. "Long-Term Effects of the Calculus Workshop Model." Final report to the National Science Foundation, NSF grant no. MDR-9150212, Washington, D.C., 1992.

Brush, S. G. "Women in Science and Engineering." *American Scientist,* 1991, 79, 404–419.

Carmichael, J. W., and Sevenair, J. P. "Preparing Minorities for Science Careers." *Issues in Science and Technology,* 1991, 7 (3), 55–60.

Carpenter, V. L., Friar, S., and Lipe, M. G. "Evidence on the Performance of Accounting Students: Race, Gender, and Expectations." *Issues in Accounting Education,* 1993, 8 (1), 1–17.

Green, K. C. "A Profile of Undergraduates in the Sciences." *American Scientist,* 1989, 77, 475–480.

Hall, R. M., and Sandler, B. "The Classroom Climate: A Chilly One for Women?" Project on the Status and Education of Women. Washington, D.C.: Association of American Colleges, 1982.

Herring, H. C., III, and Izard, C. D. "Outcomes Assessment of Accounting Majors." *Issues in Accounting Education,* 1992, 7 (1), 1–17.

Hilton, T. L., and Lee, V. E. "Student Interest and Persistence in Sciences: Changes in the Educational Pipeline in the Last Decade." *Journal of Higher Education,* 1988, *59,* 510–526.

Holland, D. C., and Eisenhart, M. A. *Educated in Romance: Women, Achievement, an College Culture.* Chicago: University of Chicago Press, 1990.

Krupnick, C. G. "Women and Men in the Classroom: Inequality and Its Remedies." *On Learning.* Cambridge, Mass.: Harvard-Danforth Center, 1984.

Levin, J., and Wyckoff, J. "Effective Advising: Identifying Students Most Likely to Persist and Succeed in Engineering." *Engineering Education,* 1988, *78,* 178–182.

National Academy of Sciences. *Nurturing Science and Engineering Talent: A Discussion Paper.* The Government–Industry Research Roundtable. Washington, D.C.: National Academy of Sciences, 1987.

Oakes, J. *Multiplying Inequalities: The Effects of Race, Social Class, and Tracking on Opportunities to Learn Mathematics and Science.* Santa Monica, Calif.: Rand Corporation, 1990.

Office of Technology Assessment. *Demographic Trends and the Scientific and Engineering Workforce.* Washington, D.C.: Office of Technology Assessment, 1985.

Rawls, R. L. "Minorities in Science." *Chemical and Engineering News,* Apr. 15, 1991, pp. 20–35.

Seymour, D. "Quality on Campus: Three Institutions, Three Beginnings." *Change,* May/June 1993, pp. 14–27.

Seymour, E. "Undergraduate Problems with Teaching and Advising in SME Majors— Explaining Gender Differences in Attrition Rates." *Journal of College Science Teaching,* Mar./Apr. 1992, pp. 284–298.

Seymour, E., and Hewitt, N. M. *Talking About Leaving: Factors Contributing to High Attrition Rates Among Science, Mathematics, and Engineering Undergraduate Majors.* Final report to the Alfred P. Sloan Foundation on an ethnographic inquiry at seven institutions. Boulder: University of Colorado Bureau of Sociological Research, 1994.

Tidball, M. E., and Kistiakowsky, V. "Baccalaureate Origins of American Scientists and Scholars." *Science,* Aug. 1976, *193,* 646–652.

Treisman, P. U. "A Study of the Mathematics Performance of Black Students at the University of California, Berkeley." Unpublished doctoral dissertation, University of California, Berkeley, 1985.

Trujillo, C. M. "A Comparative Examination of Classroom Interactions Between Professors and Minority and Nonminority College Students." *American Educational Research Journal,* 1986, *23* (4), 629–642.

Westat, Inc. *Tabulations for the Nation at Risk Update Study as Part of the 1987 High School Transcript Study.* Washington, D.C.: National Center for Education Statistics, 1987.

Widnall, S. E. "AAAS Presidential Lecture: Voices from the Pipeline." *Science,* Sept. 1988, *241,* 29–30, 1740–1745.

Witter, R. "Looking for Funds in All the Right Places." *SUMMAC Forum,* Dec. 1993, *1* (3), 2–3.

Wyer, J. C. "Change Where You Might Least Expect It: Accounting Education." *Change,* Jan./Feb. 1993, pp. 12–17.

JOANNE GAINEN is director of the Teaching and Learning Center at Santa Clara University, where she is working with faculty to develop student-led instructional support groups in high-risk courses.

This chapter examines the role of metacognition in fostering or inhibiting success in first-level courses in quantitative subjects. The author describes her efforts to build an I-can-do-it attitude in an elementary statistics course in psychology and identifies unresolved problems of student resistance to active learning methods.

So What Is the Problem? Difficulties at the Gate

Eleanor W. Willemsen

In the fall quarter of my junior year, I walked in the door of a class I had enrolled in called "The Theory of Real Variables." I was with my good friend, Sally, who had coached and encouraged me through five quarters of calculus and who had recently married a theoretical physicist. I had earned Bs in calculus but As in a yearlong mathematical statistics sequence. I thought I could do upper-division math at the same level as I had done calculus. I enjoyed studying with Sally even though I perceived her to be a "brain" who would always be able to learn technical material more quickly than I could. Sally was an engaging, outgoing, and energetic person who made the process of learning together fun.

When we entered the large old classroom, in a building on Stanford's inner quad, the professor was writing on the blackboard. He was a short man in later middle age dressed in a suit, with a serious demeanor and facial expression. The board rapidly filled up with Greek symbols, integral signs, and other esoteric detritus. Although some of these symbols were familiar (integral signs, for example), others were completely unfamiliar; to this day, I can't recall exactly what they were. Sally and I sat down quietly to fit in with the hushed, serious atmosphere in the room, which contained about twenty-five other students, all of them male (this was 1958). The professor turned to the class and said simply, "There is a syllabus on the chair in the back. Today we will discuss this theorem." With that comment, he whirled back toward the board, and began to babble incoherently (it seemed to me) in symbolic abstraction.

I stared at the board as the chalk raced across, covering it with expressions, arrows, parentheses, and underlining. At first, I struggled to "follow the train" even though it seemed confusing and swift. My mind raced ahead to thoughts of how I could slow it all down by reading the text or how I could get tutoring from Sally. But soon the moving train began to feel like a racing locomotive about to plunge over a cliff and smash on the rocky canyon floor below. That canyon was the canyon of my descent into "math phobia."

Although I had achieved a very advanced level before encountering this problem, which is familiar to many women, my experience illustrates a sequence that is common for students studying quantitative material. To this day, when I recall the scene in that classroom of so many years ago, I recall the very thoughts in my head, "This stuff makes no sense to me. This stuff will never make any sense to me no matter how hard I work. I am completely incapable of ever learning this kind of material. I am simply not smart enough to learn it."

My reaction illustrates the I-can't-do-it attitude that is all too prevalent in students who enroll in the quantitative college courses that are necessary for the professional careers they aspire to. It literally shuts down information processing. It is not a sign of inability to learn, however. Another personal story illustrates how an equally challenging situation can lead to the more positive "I can do it!" attitude.

In the fall quarter previous to the one just described, I simultaneously enrolled in an advanced statistics sequence in the psychology department and a basic mathematical statistics yearlong sequence. On the first day of the mathematical statistics class, I walked in and sat down among a group of strangers, mostly men. The professor was an energetic and enthusiastic man in his early forties who began by greeting the class warmly and handing out copies of the syllabus. Soon he was covering the board with symbols—just as the real variable professor did—but he stopped after a moment and asked if anyone had any concerns about having the background needed to follow the kind of expressions he had put on the board. I was relieved to hear him tell another student that a year of calculus was plenty. Although I had little in common with this man, I was hearing him say "If you learned calculus, you can learn this." I then started to examine the expressions on the board, and I saw some familiar patterns (row means and column means, and so on), which related to the psychological data analysis that I was learning in my other statistics class, and which I already knew something about.

About twenty minutes into the class session my feeling was "I can do this!" I left that first session feeling enthusiastic about the possibility of learning a lot more about something I already knew how to do. My confidence was bolstered when I talked with a couple of statistics graduate students who were taking the class because they had majored in other things as undergraduates. They seemed confused about the concrete aspects of the day's examples because these had referred to things like "control groups" and "treatments," terms that were familiar to me from psychology classes. We went for coffee and I explained the examples, which reinforced my sense of "knowing something" and encouraged my perception that the class would be interesting and fun. I even began to fantasize about becoming a college professor who teaches statistics (and today I am, in part, that professor). I do not know what has become of the statistics graduate students I helped, but I do know that not everyone in that class was as encouraged as I was.

The key idea I want to draw from these vignettes is that the I-can-do-it attitude is critical for a successful learning experience in a difficult quantitatively based course. Students who have this positive attitude will learn successfully in the gatekeeper classes and they will thus gain access to the fields of study that require the courses as part of the major program. For professors, the important message is that we can create this I-can attitude in minutes.

Metacognition and the I-Can-Do-It Attitude

The I-can-do-it attitude discussed in the two vignettes is an example of metacognition. Metacognition is defined by psychologists as *thinking about our own mental processes*. It includes our reflections on our own abilities, capacities for learning, and capabilities for using what we learn to address problems productively. The metacognitions that students have about their mental processes in the context of the courses they take are often most apparent in the expectations they have about how successful their learning will be. The I-can-do-it attitude—or its I-can't-do-it opposite—summarizes the student's beliefs, expectations, and emotions about his or her prospective learning experience in a particular class.

Why Metacognition Is Important. This "I can" attitude is enabling on several counts: It clarifies that quantitative skill is part of the self-concept; it motivates persistent effort in the face of possible frustration; and it infuses the classroom experience with some quality that both makes it more enjoyable and facilitates focus on the material.

Let us look further at three ways in which the I-can-do-it feeling improves the chances for a student having a successful learning experience in a difficult quantitative class. The first is through the attitude's attention-directing effect. A belief in one's own capability lends positive affect to the class material and serves therefore to help direct attention to the material instead of to counterproductive negative "self-talk" (Bandura, 1986). Students who drop math, statistics, and natural science classes often do so because their first experiences with solving problems or reading about how to do so in the text stimulate reactions such as "Oh, this is so difficult; I'll never be able to get it" or "I have never been any good at these kinds of problems" or even, as in my first story, "I am completely incapable of learning this material." Such negative expectations are examples of what psychologists call a "negative attributional style." Outcomes of learning efforts are attributed to one's talent or presumed lack of talent. They focus attention on the self—on negative self-evaluation at that—and are incompatible with a receptive attitude toward the material on the board or in the text. In contrast, when a positive and enabling attitude is present, the student can receive and think about the course material itself.

The second way in which the I-can-do-it attitude facilitates mastery of difficult course material is by making it possible for the student to persist in the face of the inevitable frustration that comes in tackling new material and trying to master the skills needed to deal with it. Skills are not always acquired quickly, and working on problems that seem unsolvable can indeed generate anxiety. What the "I can" feeling contributes is the sense that repeated—even tedious—efforts will be productive; in other words, it contributes an expectation of learning and mastery. This expectation represents a style of attribution that contrasts with the attribution to talent discussed earlier (Dweck and Elliott, 1983). The expectation of eventual success keeps the student going when first attempts at homework problems fail or when the professor's scratching on the board is not immediately meaningful. My own experience was that many more example problems were needed for me to learn each important calculus concept than were needed for Sally, but I cheerfully persisted because I believed that mastery would result. And it did.

The third way that learning in a classroom is facilitated by the "I can" attitude is related to the social climate that is created when students are optimistic about their abilities to learn. They expect to share a common emotional experience as well as an intellectual one. They are thus more likely to perceive the people around them as fellow learners whose efforts are similar to their own (Seligman, 1991). Most of us have a tendency to think that others know how to deal with ambiguous or tough situations better than we do. But when students sharing an experience feel competent in its domain, they can see themselves as more similar to those other, presumably competent, classmates. When students attribute learning to talent, they are likely to focus on differences between themselves and others. When effort is seen as the basis for learning, they can all see they have potential.

Taken together, these effects of a positive attitude—the material is seen positively, the frustration of learning is overcome through persistence, and a sense of commonality among students is created—have a synergistic effect. When a student focuses on course material, works hard on examples, and sees that there are multiple perspectives among fellow learners, it is more likely that he or she will make generalizations about the problems and find helpful approaches to them. Thoughts about how to approach problems are an important kind of metacognition that facilitates putting learning into professional practice.

We all may readily agree that it is important to help students develop and sustain an I-can-do-it attitude in our classes, but we are equally likely to agree that there are a number of barriers to doing so. Let us examine now the factors that influence the development of this positive attitude with a focus on those we can affect through our teaching.

Influences on Students' Metacognitive Attitudes About Learning

Students carry into their classrooms certain ideas, beliefs, memories, and attitudes that powerfully influence what each of them experiences once the class begins. Among the most powerful of these internalized beliefs is that teachers know the subject and are responsible for transmitting it—what Perry calls the "dualistic" view (Perry, 1970). It can also be thought of as the perspective of "received knowing" (Belenky, Clinchy, Goldberger, and Tarule, 1986). To relate it to the main thesis of this chapter, this student belief can be likened to a metacognition of learning as getting material out of the teacher's head and into one's own head.

This belief promotes a very passive style on the student's part. It leads to a pattern of more and more notes, a focus on facts and details instead of concepts, and a tendency toward less and less thinking—in sum, an "I don't know what to do" attitude toward problems. In essence, this is a "Teacher can do it" attitude as opposed to an "I can do it" attitude. Students expect that if they can follow along the steps being shown by the teacher this means they have learned the material. Both teacher and student are thus disappointed when, after the first quiz or challenging problem set, it becomes apparent that they have not. As teachers, we are tempted to attribute this failure to the students' lack of effort, but to do so is to adopt a "they can't do it" attitude that will not help us very much as we try to facilitate learning. I will return to this point a little later during the discussion of facilitating positive cognition.

Another factor influencing students' metacognitions about a class is their memories of past experiences with quantitative or other challenging material. If these memories are negative, there is a strong barrier to empowerment. A series of frustrating experiences, when the student received poor grades or failed to learn according to his or her own expectations, may have created a sense of "learned helplessness," that is, the "I can't do it" attitude (see Seligman, 1991). This attitude may lead to anxiety every time the student approaches this kind of material and will, in turn, make it difficult for the student to concentrate on it and organize an appropriate cognitive framework.

I call memories about past experiences with quantitative material metacognitive histories. When a student's metacognitive histories are negative, the student may not have formed the kinds of detailed insights into his or her own learning that other students have. A student who has had a history of successful learning with quantitative material will often have formed some ideas about his or her own learning process. "I need to do lots of example problems before I can get it," or "The best approach for me is to have my friend show me the steps she used," or "It always helps me to start with a list of what I know and what I need to solve for," are examples of helpful metacognitions. The absence of helpful metacognitions is a barrier to a positive attitude. Students without these kinds of insights lack an important resource to guide them in solving problems. More importantly, these kinds of insights can contribute to their sense that there is a predictable sequence in which learning will occur. The absence of such metacognitions thus can be a barrier to learning.

The second class of barriers to the I-can-do-it attitude come from the interpersonal relationships and interactions that surround the learning experience. A professor who is remote and seems unapproachable poses a barrier.

The interpersonal transaction between professor and student is critical. When the professor engages the student in personal conversation, recognizes her by name, and seems to include her in the domain of attention, the subject matter seems more accessible. The nonverbal message goes out that the student is a part of the community of people who can do mathematics, statistics, chemistry, or whatever the subject is. Of course, the interpersonal relation between teacher and student can be counterproductive as well, and, when it is, a powerful barrier to further learning is created.

I recall an interaction with a professor on the first day of one of my statistics classes. He looked at me as I stood by the table in the front of the classroom, which was filled to capacity with male students, many of them graduate students. "Women can't learn this material," he announced off into space somewhere past my face. He then turned to his notes, and only when I persisted in standing there did he hastily jot a signature on the form I needed to add his class.

The message I got in that statistics class that day was that I was *not* part of the community of that class and that the professor could not imagine my ever being part of his world—a world made up of mathematically sophisticated applied scientists who worked with complex formulas to address interesting problems. Luckily, my friend Sally joined me in the class and we were able to support each other during the term. Those were the days just before the Betty Friedan book that started the women's movement in the United States (Friedan, 1963). We did not immediately think about sexism and bias. We merely thought the man was silly. Through supporting each other, working and studying together, and sharing a heightened sense of challenge, we were able to learn the subject so well that we got the highest two grades in the class. We knew this from the posted class distribution, but the professor said nothing about it when we came in together to pick up our exams.

Peer support and connection can be a powerful boost to learning, and its absence can be a major barrier. When students feel different from and distant from the other students in the room, thoughts of "They can, I can't" can easily create a barrier.

The organization and structure of the course itself can also create sense of distance between the student and the subject matter. Quantitatively oriented courses are often presented with a "bottom line" flavor. What matters are correct answers, getting good quiz grades, getting the solutions to the problems, and so on. Although solutions do, of course, matter, an emphasis on them in the syllabus and in handouts may obscure the importance of the process needed to learn how to get to the concepts that help us think about the problems and, ultimately, solve them. Students may then be envisioning a process in which they cannot participate.

Another component of class structure that serves as a barrier is the use of problems and examples taken out of the context (laboratory studies, clinical interviews, larger data analysis tasks, and so on) in which they would naturally occur. These problems seem unfamiliar and remote from anything the student finds meaningful. A well-established principle of learning is that meaningful material is easier to learn than unfamiliar and less meaningful material (Brown, Bransford, Ferrara, and Campione, 1983).

Overcoming the Barriers: An Approach to Elementary Statistics

For several terms, I have been experimenting with an approach to the elementary statistics class that is designed to foster the I-can attitude. The approach is intended to overcome the barriers to a positive attitude and to facilitate the learning of skills and their applications.

First, the syllabus is organized around approximately ten key ideas in statistical reasoning—for example, "Variability is a basic and measurable (estimable) characteristic of any group of scores" or "A set of scores is more easily understood when visualized." This organization around a few simple ideas is intended to help students experience statistical thinking as they would any other kind of thinking.

A second component—collaborative group work during the class meetings—addresses several goals, including learning by doing, reflecting on problem-solving approaches, and clarifying through communicating.

A third component is the use of the students' own scores on a dozen personality variables. This capitalizes on the motivating characteristics of self-generated and self-referent data (Rogers, Kuiper, and Kirker, 1977).

An additional component is a requirement that each group generate two complete "minireports," following the editorial style of the American Psychological Association. These reports require groups to select data from the class set, analyze it with a simple software package (MYSTAT), and interpret it. This activity promotes reflection on data analysis and the synthesis of and communication about several such analyses.

Because I have designed this course based on my creative reflections about the barriers to an I-can-do-it attitude, it works wonders and everybody learns . . . right? Unfortunately, wrong. Let me describe some of my experiences with the course in order to understand the problems that must be carefully and persistently addressed if we wish to empower students to learn difficult material.

Students are generally positive at first and, indeed, they enjoy discussing their "personalities" with one another and doing the other group activities described. However, after several sessions, students resume a more passive attitude during the supposedly "active learning" periods. "What shall we do? Can you give us a list of steps? Is this the right approach?" they ask. The active learning tasks I introduce become "just homework." The personality test scores become another bunch of numbers to crunch. In a group that is not facilitated by an instructor or a peer leader, one student often becomes the role model. This strong student's work is then imitated by others, and he or she becomes the "one who knows." The others, then, are likely to think of themselves as "the ones who don't know."

To get everybody thinking, I sometimes ask groups to visualize data by using one of the graphic tools we have studied along with a one-sentence report to the class about their display. Or I may ask them to summarize it in a written paragraph. Writing thus becomes a tool for pushing them to think their work through and reflect on its meaning. There is often a lot of resistance to writing and visualizing. "I got it right; I just don't know what you want me to say about it" is a common refrain. I must work to overcome the dichotomous thinking that sets apart writing and math in students' minds. Expressing what they have learned from a problem carried through to completion is often just the stimulus needed to produce the I-can-do-it feeling.

On the whole, teaching this revised introductory statistics course has been rewarding. Students have been positive about their own learning, and they seem to form a habit of working with others that I see them carrying into other classes. Demand is growing for the optional advanced course in statistics, which is largely run as a single collaborative independent study group.

The authors of other chapters in this book explore some approaches to overcoming barriers to students' feelings of empowerment toward learning challenging quantitative and technical material. Some of the approaches explicitly address problems such as the ones I have just been discussing. Joanne Gainen and I return to this statistics course in Chapter Ten, and we draw from the wisdom offered by the other authors to develop a new approach to overcome the problems I have just outlined.

References

Bandura, A. *Social Foundations of Thought and Action: A Social Cognitive Theory.* Englewood Cliffs, N.J.: Prentice Hall, 1986.

Belenky, M. F., Clinchy, B. M., Goldberger, N. R., and Tarule, J. M. *Women's Ways of Knowing: The Development of Self, Voice, and Mind.* New York: Basic Books, 1986.

Brown, A. L., Bradsford, J. D., Ferrara, R. A., and Campione, J. C. "Learning, Remembering and Understanding." In J. H. Flavell and E. M. Markman (eds.), *Handbook of Child Psychology.* Vol. 3. New York: Wiley, 1983.

Dweck, C. S., and Elliott, E. S. "Achievement Motivation." In E. M. Hetherington (ed.), *Handbook of Child Psychology.* Vol. 4. New York: Wiley, 1983.

Friedan, B. *The Feminine Mystique.* New York: Norton, 1963.

Perry, W. G., Jr. *Forms of Intellectual and Ethical Development in the College Years: A Scheme.* Troy, Mo.: Holt, Rinehart & Winston, 1970.

Rogers, T. B., Kuiper, N. A., and Kirker, W. S. "Self-Reference and the Encoding of Personal Information." *Journal of Personality and Social Psychology,* 1977, 35, 677–688.

Seligman, M.E.P. *Learned Optimism.* New York: Knopf, 1991.

ELEANOR W. WILLEMSEN is professor of psychology at Santa Clara University, where she uses active learning methods to teach statistics and developmental psychology and where she conducts research on attachment.

The Academic Excellence Workshop demonstrates that achievement of underrepresented minority students in mathematics and subsequent persistence in SME majors may be associated less with precollege ability than with in-college academic experiences and expectations.

Increasing Minority Students' Success in Calculus

Martin Vern Bonsangue, David Eli Drew

During the past ten years the undergraduate calculus course has attracted an unprecedented level of national interest. Since the release of the David Report (David, 1984) concerning the state of undergraduate and graduate mathematics in this country, the National Science Foundation has spent more than $5 million on programs to strengthen the calculus. Professional organizations such as the Mathematical Association of America (MAA) and the American Mathematical Association of Two Year Colleges (AMATYC) have regularly included in their professional meetings sessions on "calculus reform" and "the first two years." Indeed, about a quarter of the sessions at the 1993 annual joint meetings of the American Mathematical Society/Mathematical Association of America conference dealt with undergraduate mathematics education. Although both opinions and practices of teaching the calculus vary widely, the calculus reform movement has affected nearly every two-year and four-year college and university in America (Steen, 1987).

Among the most widely recognized intervention programs in college mathematics is the calculus workshop model that was developed for African American students at the University of California, Berkeley by Uri Treisman in the late 1970s (American Mathematical Society, 1988; Fullilove and Treisman, 1990; Selvin, 1992; Treisman, 1985). The Berkeley model, known now as the Emerging Scholars Program (ESP), has been adapted in mathematics courses at more than a dozen major universities across the country (Selvin, 1992), with

This project was supported by the National Science Foundation, grant no. MDR-9150212. Opinions expressed are those of the authors and not necessarily those of the foundation.

more than a hundred two-year and four-year colleges initiating trial ESP-type programs in the past five years. In a recent issue examining pipeline issues for minority students in science, mathematics, or engineering (SME) majors ("Minorities in Science . . . ," 1992), *Science* reported that some ESP programs have dramatically lowered dropout rates and increased the number of minority students majoring in SME fields. For example, the graduate program in applied mathematics at Rice University and the undergraduate mathematics program at the University of Texas at Austin each award approximately one-fourth of their degrees to African American or Latino/Latina students (Selvin, 1992). In 1992, Treisman received a MacArthur Award for this work, in recognition of its national impact on the success of underrepresented minority students in mathematics-based fields.

Purpose of the Research

The present research represents the first longitudinal investigation of the effects of workshop participation on persistence and achievement of underrepresented minority students enrolled in mathematics, science, and engineering majors. The study also investigates students' interpretations of the effect of their workshop experience on their academic performance and academic choices. The study is based on the workshop model implemented at the California State Polytechnic University, Pomona (Cal Poly), a comprehensive state university that is recognized for its achievement in technical fields. This study extends the Berkeley report in three ways. First, the study considers the efficacy of the workshop model in an academic setting different in goals and selectivity from Berkeley; second, the study examines the effectiveness of the model for other underrepresented groups (primarily Latinos); and third, the study traces the effects of the workshop experience over a significant period of time.

The Academic Excellence Workshop Program at Cal Poly

The Academic Excellence Workshop (AEW) program at Cal Poly is jointly sponsored by the College of Engineering and the College of Science. The workshop program began in fall 1986 with one section of first-year calculus. Although the present study considered only the performance of students in calculus, the AEW now includes workshops in chemistry, physics, and mechanical engineering. From fall 1986 to fall 1991, ninety-five different workshops have enrolled more than one thousand student participants.

The Academic Excellence Workshop program, like the Berkeley model, is premised upon excellence in student performance rather than remediation. The Cal Poly program targets Native American, African American, and Latino/Latina students. The purpose of the program is to build community and academic involvement among its constituents, with the ultimate goal of persistence and completion of an engineering or science degree (Academic Excellence Workshops, 1992).

Upon acceptance to the College of Science or Engineering, each African American, Latino/Latina, and Native American student received a letter and personal telephone call from a faculty member or student workshop leader inviting her or him to attend an informational meeting explaining the Academic Excellence Workshop program. Approximately half of the students who were contacted chose to participate in a workshop session for one, two, or three quarters of calculus. White and Asian American students were not eligible to participate in the program, although several students were allowed to join as "guests." The "workshop group" in the present study refers to the underrepresented minority students who participated in the workshop for one or more quarters.

The structure of the workshops was similar to that of the Berkeley program. Each student was enrolled in a traditional lecture section of calculus that included workshop and nonworkshop students of all ethnic groups. Unlike the large lectures at Berkeley, the classes averaged about thirty-five students and met for four hours per week. Since there was no recitation section attached to the course, student questions about homework problems and the like were covered in class by the instructor. Workshop and nonworkshop students were responsible for the same classwork, homework, and examinations.

In addition to attending the lecture class, workshop students met in structured groups of ten to twelve students twice a week for two-hour sessions outside of class to work collaboratively on calculus problems. Group leaders, or facilitators, represented mainly by upper-division minority undergraduate SME students, directed the problem-solving activities by constructing worksheets with calculus problems that helped reinforce concepts or expose weaknesses in the students' levels of understanding (see Treisman, 1985, pp. 42–44; Bonsangue, 1992, p. 279). The expectation, which was made clear to workshop students, was that they would excel in, rather than just get through, the course. A typical worksheet problem reviewing exponential growth as follows:

> Agronomists use the assumption that one-quarter acre of land is required to provide food for one person and estimate that there are 10 billion acres of tillable land in the world, so a maximum of 40 billion people can be sustained if no other food source is available. The world population in the beginning of 1980 was approximately 4.5 billion. Assuming the population increases at a rate of 2 percent per year, when will the maximum sustainable population be reached?

During the first half hour of the workshop session, students usually worked alone. Gradually, they began discussing the problems and comparing solutions. After an hour, the sessions became quite lively, with students explaining their solutions and interpretations to one another. The facilitator then could help individual students or direct the discussion of the group questions that arose. (The course instructor wrote the exams used in her or his course, so the facilitator had no information about exam questions.) The sessions also had an informal social aspect, with students sometimes munching on popcorn or pizza while they worked. Moreover, the discussions often included nonmathematical topics as well, such as information on future course sign-ups or deadlines, upcoming departmental activities, or personal concerns.

Role of the Facilitator. The leader or facilitator, often a former workshop participant, was an undergraduate science or engineering major who had received special training by the Colleges of Science and Engineering in leading workshop sessions (see Academic Excellence Workshops, 1992). Unlike a tutor, the facilitator's primary role was to initiate and sustain interaction between workshop students by providing challenging and relevant problems. The facilitator usually did not respond to questions with direct answers but tried to foster a dialogue with the group. The goal of the workshop was to involve students in substantive mathematical or scientific problem-solving discussions with their peers. Workshop students were not permitted to do homework during the sessions. Rather, students understood that the worksheets done in the session were in addition to the regular homework assignments given in class.

The facilitator met weekly for several hours with the workshop program director and other facilitators to develop good worksheet problems and discuss concerns. He or she also met briefly once a week with the course instructor to ensure that the worksheet problems were relevant and appropriate to that week's lesson, and to verify class attendance of workshop students. The facilitator contacted the student after more than one successive absence from either the lecture or the workshop. The facilitator was therefore often the first to become aware of students' personal, financial, or logistical problems. Often these problems were resolved in a timely way with the help of the facilitator, other students, the instructor, or the workshop director. Thus, for many students, the workshop facilitator served as the critical academic and personal hook for initial and continued success in the course. The role and job description for workshop facilitators are detailed in the *Handbook for Academic Excellence Workshops* (Academic Excellence Workshops, 1992).

Research Findings

The characteristics and performance of Cal Poly students majoring in SME was followed over a five-year period, from 1986 to 1991.

Sample Characteristics. The workshop sample was composed of 133 Latino/Latina and African American students who participated in at least one calculus workshop section while enrolled in a traditional lecture calculus section. The performance of this group was compared with that of three peer groups of students enrolled in the same lecture sections of first-quarter calculus. These included 187 African American and Latino/Latina students not enrolled in the workshop, 208 white, non-Latino/Latina students, and 198 Asian or Pacific Island students, for a total sample of 726 students. The workshop sample was composed primarily of Latino/Latina students (116 were men, 133 were women); about one-fourth of the workshop students overall were women (36/133). The nonworkshop minority group was composed mostly of Latino/Latina students (159/187), and 21 percent of the total group were women. Both the white and Asian American comparison groups had a slightly larger percentage of women (30 percent).

Precollege Achievement Measures. The academic preparation of workshop and nonworkshop students was compared using SAT-Math, SAT-Verbal, high school grade-point average (HSGPA), and the student's score on the department's precalculus placement exam. There were no statistically significant differences between the minority workshop and minority nonworkshop groups in any of the four precollege academic measures. Likewise, there were no differences between white and Asian American students in SAT-M, HSGPA, or placement exam scores, although Asian American students scored slightly lower in SAT-V. African American and Latino/Latina students scored significantly lower on SAT-M and on the placement exam than did the white and Asian American group. High school GPAs were almost identical for all groups, with a mean of 3.33 for all students.

Thus, for this sample, students' selection into the Academic Excellence Workshop program was not associated with precollege achievement. However, the underrepresented minority students began their calculus sequence with lower measures of mathematics achievement than did their nonminority peers. Interpreting high school GPA as a measure of exposure suggests that none of the four groups had an initial advantage in adapting to the rigors of a university-level calculus course.

Results for Workshop and Nonworkshop Minority Groups. Although African American and Latino/Latina workshop students had no initial advantage in mathematics background or achievement over their nonworkshop peers, these students achieved a mean grade of more than six-tenths of a grade point above nonworkshop students in first- and second-year calculus. Moreover, within three years of entering the institution, 52 percent of the nonworkshop minority students had either withdrawn from the institution or changed to a nonmathematics-based major, compared with 15 percent of the workshop students. Furthermore, as a result of course failure, nonworkshop students required an average of one full quarter more to complete their three-quarter calculus sequence. Individual records showed high patterns of course-repeating, with nearly half (46 percent) of the nonworkshop minority students requiring five or more quarters to complete a three-quarter calculus sequence, compared with fewer than one-fifth (17 percent) of the workshop students. Moreover, 91 percent of the workshop students still enrolled in SME majors after three years had completed their mathematics requirement in their respective SME majors, compared with just 58 percent of the nonworkshop minority students (see Figure 3.1). These statistically significant differences were also found when comparing Latino/Latina workshop students along with their nonworkshop counterparts.

Figure 3.1. Persistence in SME Courses by Minority Students

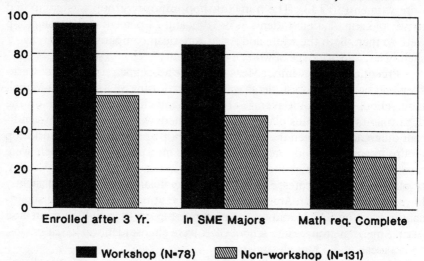

The association of workshop participation with academic success and persistence was particularly strong among minority women, all of whom were Latina in this sample. All twenty-two of the women who had taken the calculus workshop were still enrolled at Cal Poly after three years, with nineteen (86 percent) remaining in a mathematics-based major. Of these, each had completed her mathematics requirement and was eligible for graduation. In contrast, only twelve (52 percent) of the original group of twenty-three nonworkshop minority women were still enrolled after three years. Further, only four of the original cohort of twenty-three nonworkshop women successfully completed her mathematics requirement and was eligible for graduation. These differences occurred even though no initial academic advantage was found for either group on precollege measures such as SAT-Math, SAT-Verbal, and HSGPA.

Comparison with White and Asian American Nonworkshop Groups. In the first-year and second-year calculus sequence, African American and Latino/Latina workshop students achieved the same grades as white students and slightly (but not significantly) lower grades than Asian American students. After three years, 50 percent of nonworkshop white students and 41 percent of nonworkshop Asian American students had withdrawn from the SME major or left the institution, compared with 15 percent of the workshop students. The pattern of repeating courses was almost identical for nonminority nonworkshop groups and workshop students, with each group averaging about 3.7 quarters to complete the three-quarter sequence. White and Asian American women had SME attrition rates of 38 percent and 45 percent, respectively, while those for white and Asian American men were 55 percent and 39 percent, respectively. Of the nonworkshop students who persisted in SME majors, 82 percent of whites and 89 percent of Asian Americans had completed their mathematics requirement within three years, proportions that were similar to the 91 percent completion rate for African American and Latino/Latina workshop students.

Skimming and Self-Selection. The data reported in the previous section show that African American and Latino/Latina students who participated in the workshop calculus sessions achieved at levels as high as or higher than any other ethnic group, both during the first (workshop) year and afterward. Although social and personal factors undoubtedly influenced their achievement and persistence, this study found that traditional measures of precollege achievement were not associated with student success (see Bonsangue and Drew, 1992, or Bonsangue, 1994, for a more complete discussion).

The critical issue of self-selection cannot be fully addressed in this study because students were not randomly assigned to workshop or nonworkshop groups. However, the study did find evidence that calculus achievement for workshop students was, at least in part, a result of developing student talent rather than merely "skimming," or selecting and cultivating the most talented students. First, as noted earlier, precollege measures for workshop students were no higher—and were sometimes lower—than those of nonworkshop students. Second, a comparison of the grades of minority students enrolled in first-quarter calculus sections before and after the inception of the workshop revealed no change in average performance for the nonworkshop group compared with students in earlier, traditionally taught sections (see Figure 3.2). If the best students were selected into the workshop, we would expect the performance of the nonworkshop group to have declined. Before the workshop in 1986, minority students achieved a mean calculus grade of below 1.7, or D+. After 1986, the average performance of all minority students, both workshop and nonworkshop, rose more than two-tenths of a grade point, a statistically significant gain, surpassing the overall performance of white students in the sample.

**Figure 3.2. Calculus 1 Performance,
Underrepresented Minority Students**

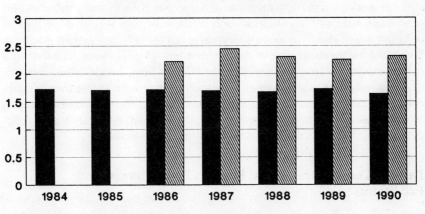

Student Experiences of the Program

Workshop students from the 1987–88 cohorts were interviewed to explore their perceptions of how their workshop involvement may have affected their academic patterns and self-perceptions. Seventy percent of the interviewees reported that they would not have done as well in their calculus courses had they not been in a workshop. This perception was especially strong among women.

The majority of workshop students reported two lasting effects of the workshop: (1) an early awareness of the academic expectations in technical courses, and (2) a recognition of the need to remain connected to their student peers, professors, and academic advisers throughout their college careers. Many students reported their initial surprise or even shock at the expectations and competition levels they experienced during their first year at Cal Poly. They associated their successful transition to college-level mathematics with their workshop experience. Drawing upon that experience, half of the students interviewed indicated that they have since regularly formed study groups in their upper-division courses, perhaps helping to account for their success in completing advanced mathematics requirements.

Gender and Minority Issues. Reports such as those of the National Research Council (1989, 1990) and "Minorities in Science . . ." (1992) have helped increase awareness of the disproportional failure of underrepresented groups (ethnic groups, gender groups, age groups, and disabled groups) of students. This study found some evidence of feelings of ethnic separation and academic inadequacy among those minority students interviewed in spite of their success in the program. However, feelings of exclusion and inadequacy seemed to be centered primarily on gender rather than ethnic issues.

Even though the workshop program was not designed to address gender issues, the most compelling results were those for women in the workshop. The Latina women enrolled in the workshop, of all ethnic and gender groups, had the highest persistence rate in the university and in their MSE majors. The nine women who were interviewed (see Bonsangue, 1994) indicated a direct effect of workshop participation on their success, both in study patterns and peer relationships. Nonetheless, each of these women reported feelings of isolation or self-doubt in varying degrees, even though they earned grades as high as or higher than those of their male peers. Overall, women described a college experience that was qualitatively different from that described by men. The relatively high attrition rates of nonminority women (more than 40 percent) may indicate that they, too, experience such feelings in technical courses. However, in the workshop program, minority women evidently found sufficient support to offset these negative feelings and to persist.

Passing Through the Gates: Benefits for Undergraduate Facilitators

One of the most significant effects of the Academic Excellence Workshop involves the benefits for undergraduates who served as facilitators in the program. Between 1991 and 1993, at least fifteen Latino/Latina and African American facilitators were accepted at graduate or medical schools, more than triple the number of such acceptances over a three-year period before inception of the workshop. One possible explanation is the increased level of performance of facilitators on graduate entry exams such as the GRE and MCAT, especially for students who were workshop facilitators in chemistry and physics courses. Informal interviews with these students indicate that in facilitating these science courses, they felt that they mastered the material that provided a solid basis to score well on the graduate exams. Several students mentioned that they were planning to pursue doctoral degrees and teach at the university level, a new professional interest that was triggered by their workshop experience.

Analysis of Program Cost

The Course Attempt Ratio (CAR) was introduced as a measure of initial success and program efficiency. The CAR is defined as the ratio of the number of times a student attempted a course or series of courses to the number of courses successfully completed. Ideally, the CAR for a course is 1.00. CARs can be computed for an individual student or for a group of students for one or more courses. The workshop group had a CAR of 1.19 for first-quarter calculus, compared with 1.43 for nonworkshop minority students. Statistically significant differences in CARs were found between workshop and nonworkshop students in each of the first-year courses. For the three-quarter calculus sequence, the CAR for workshop students was 3.63 compared with 4.64 for nonworkshop students—a difference of one full course for the yearlong sequence (Bonsangue and Drew, 1992).

The financial implications of these results are significant. In a state institution, part of the cost of students' enrollment is borne by the university (and ultimately, the state). When students require an extra quarter to complete the basic calculus sequence, the university must absorb that part of the cost of the extra quarter not covered by the student's tuition. An intervention program that significantly reduces the CAR for a group of students could be cost-effective if the costs associated with the program are less than that for the student to repeat a course. An analysis of the costs for the Cal Poly program indicated that in fact costs to the institution were reduced by a third for students who participated in the workshop compared with their nonworkshop peers (Bonsangue and Drew, 1992). Savings of this magnitude are potentially significant for a state institution with a strong technical and scientific orientation and a desire to increase the number of students who persist in SME majors (Bonsangue and Drew, 1992).

Conclusion

The present research investigated the effects of participation in an academic excellence workshop program on achievement and persistence among underrepresented minority students in mathematics, science, and engineering disciplines. The study found that an intervention program promoting academic excellence and meaningful peer interaction can have a direct impact on student performance not only in entry-level mathematics courses but also in subsequent courses, thereby validating recommendations of the National Research Council and others (National Research Council, 1989, 1990; Weissglass, 1992).

The findings on persistence, performance, and cost obtained from this longitudinal study underscore the need for academic institutions to have the facility to track accurately the academic performance of their students across time. The longitudinal analysis of course-repeating patterns for workshop and nonworkshop students indicated that a highly academic intervention program could be both time- and cost-effective for both the student and the institution, particularly if implemented early in the student's college career.

Questions remain about the effects of self-selectivity and the efficacy of requiring student participation in academically intensive programs. However, the Cal Poly workshop experience showed that a nontrivial number of students participated, succeeded, and formed the nucleus of a successful group of minority students in mathematics-based disciplines that currently have little minority representation. In summary, this study found that achievement among underrepresented minority students in mathematics, science, and engineering disciplines may be less associated with precollege ability than with in-college academic experiences and expectations.

References

Academic Excellence Workshops. *A Handbook for Academic Excellence Workshops*. Pomona, Calif.: Minority Engineering Program and Science Educational Enhancement Services, 1992.

American Mathematical Society. "Research in Mathematics Education." *AMS Notices*, 1988, 35(8), 1123–1131.

Bonsangue, M. "The Effects of Calculus Workshop Groups on Minority Achievement and Persistence in Mathematics, Science, and Engineering." Unpublished doctoral dissertation, Claremont Graduate School, Claremont, California, 1992.

Bonsangue, M. "An Efficacy Study of the Calculus Workshop Model." *BMS issues in Mathematics Education*. Vol. 4. Washington, D.C., 1994.

Bonsangue, M., and Drew, D. E. "Long-Term Effects of the Calculus Workshop Model." Final report to the National Science Foundation, NSF grant no. MDR-9150212, Washington, D.C., 1992.

David, E. E. *Renewing U.S. Mathematics: Critical Resource for the Future*. Washington, D.C.: National Academy Press, 1984.

Fullilove, R. E., and Treisman, P. U. "Mathematics Achievement Among African American Undergraduates at the University of California, Berkeley: An Evaluation of the Mathematics Workshop Program." *Journal of Negro Education*, 1990, 59(3), 463–7478.

"Minorities in Science: The Pipeline Problem." *Science*, Nov. 13, 1992, 258 (entire issue).

National Research Council. *Everybody Counts: A Report to the Nation on the Future of Mathematics Education*. Washington, D.C.: National Academy Press, 1989.

National Research Council. *A Challenge of Numbers: People in the Mathematical Sciences*. Washington, D.C.: National Academy Press 1990.

Selvin, P. "Math Education: Multiplying the Meager Numbers." *Science,* 1992, *258,* 1200–1201.

Steen, L. A. (ed.). *Calculus for a New Century: A Pump, Not a Filter.* Washington, D.C.: Mathematical Association of America, 1987.

Treisman, P. U. "A Study of the Mathematics Performance of Black Students at the University of California, Berkeley." Unpublished doctoral dissertation, University of California, Berkeley, 1985.

Weissglass, J. "Changing the System Means Changing Ourselves." *Education Week,* Jun. 10, 1992, pp. 28, 36.

MARTIN VERN BONSANGUE *is associate professor of mathematics at Sonoma State University. For the past three years he has conducted independent evaluations of workshop programs.*

DAVID ELI DREW *is professor of education and executive management and director of the Center for Educational Studies at the Claremont Graduate School. He conducts research on funding and evaluation of university scientific research capabilities.*

Students taking general chemistry at the College of the Holy Cross participate in a teaching and learning experience that parallels the scientific method itself. Cooperative efforts by the students in both obtaining and evaluating data support what we call "discovery chemistry," a curriculum that features introduction of many general chemistry concepts in the laboratory rather than in the lecture.

Discovery Chemistry: A Laboratory-Based Approach to General Chemistry

Mauri A. Ditzler, Robert W. Ricci

College students often see chemistry as a collection of facts and theories rather than an ongoing, participatory process for creating knowledge. Too many believe their ability to benefit from or contribute to introductory chemistry courses is determined by the factual foundation they bring from high school. Few first-year students see chemistry as a field that will allow them to develop and express their intellectual creativity. To counter this perception, chemistry faculty nationwide are engaged in a concerted effort to develop introductory courses that present chemistry as a dynamic and developing discipline that values both creativity and collaboration.

At the College of the Holy Cross (Worcester, Mass.), the chemistry department has been experimenting since 1989 with a laboratory-based, process-oriented curriculum called "discovery chemistry" (Ricci and Ditzler, 1991; Ditzler and Ricci, 1994; Jarret and McMaster, in press). Our approach is based on the philosophy that the approach to teaching chemistry should parallel the chemist's approach to investigating nature. Practicing chemists draw heavily from a widely accepted body of knowledge, making extensive use of the literature and their colleagues' expertise. In the end, however, the proof is provided by experimental evidence. In a similar fashion, the discovery chemistry program focuses the learning experience on laboratory exercises that use a guided-inquiry format. In these exercises students work individually and cooperatively to generate data that is pooled and analyzed to discover fundamental aspects of the discipline. Although discovery chemistry is novel in that it places the student within a community that actively creates knowledge from well-crafted experiments, it still draws heavily on traditional instructional tools such as lectures and textbook assignments. Furthermore, the instructor plays an active role, ensuring that students are exposed to the same processes and structure that scientists use to support their creative insights.

Rationale for a Guided-Inquiry Instructional Format

A number of well-grounded educational reasons support teaching chemistry from a guided-inquiry approach.

Exposing Students to Disciplinary Processes. Only a small fraction of the students enrolled in an introductory chemistry course become practicing chemists. Many, in fact, will have few occasions to make use of the concepts and theories they learn. For these students the course should be structured to illustrate the chemist's approach to asking and answering questions. Of course, there is also value in having these students learn fundamental theories. This second objective is important and can be accomplished in a manner that supports our goal of teaching a way of knowing. Furthermore, for those students considering a career in science, it is crucial that early courses accurately reflect the dynamic nature of chemistry, presenting it as a field that allows for expression of creativity.

Building on Faculty Expertise. College and university faculty are normally expected to balance classroom instruction and scholarly activities. Because expertise in the latter is more easily identified, faculty are often selected on the basis of their promise for research in the discipline. A teaching curriculum that focuses on carrying out and interpreting experiments merges the two activities, which are sometimes seen to be in opposition. Both students and faculty benefit because the strengths of the teacher-scholar are effectively utilized.

Using Instructional Time Efficiently. In most introductory chemistry courses students are required to spend three to four hours each week in the laboratory, often exceeding the time spent in lecture and, unfortunately, possibly even exceeding the time spent on homework. In addition, laboratory sections are generally smaller than lecture sections and are better suited for interactive and collaborative learning strategies. Consequently, the weekly laboratory exercise represents a significant portion of available instructional time and, in many ways, the most student-friendly environment available.

Accommodating Student Diversity. Introductory chemistry courses are widely recognized as gateway or gatekeeper courses. They serve as prerequisites or entryways into many scientific and health-related careers. Because chemistry has a vertical structure, students not ready for a traditional chemistry course when they enter college may be permanently denied an opportunity to study for these careers.

Because students come to college with different high school backgrounds, the content of general chemistry is more familiar to some than to others. An important feature of the laboratory-based inquiry approach is that many topics can be presented in a frame of reference that makes them appear equally new to all students. Even the topics most familiar to well-prepared students—such as the mole concept and limiting reagent problems—are not immediately recognized when introduced in a laboratory environment. First-year college students are rarely able to relate facts and theories from an earlier high school chemistry course to the phenomenological reality of the laboratory. They do not tend to predict correctly the outcome of an experiment and are not able to relate easily empirical observations to previous knowledge. Consequently, a laboratory-driven course of the type discussed in this chapter serves to level the playing field for all students. The better-prepared students benefit by having a course that holds their interest and challenges them intellectually. The poorly prepared students experience the rewards and encouragement of contributing on a more equal basis. And, finally, the instructor can better judge the level of his or her presentation since student performance is more closely tied to the current course.

A Model for Laboratory-Based Chemistry Instruction

At the College of the Holy Cross a series of one-week modules introduces the fundamentals of chemistry. Each module begins with a discovery exercise that consists of a mix between discussion and experimentation.

Organization of a Discovery Exercise. A typical discovery exercise contains three parts.

First, there is a *prelaboratory discussion*. Here the exercise is introduced in the form of a question. Although the students are given considerable freedom in making predictions, offering hypotheses, and ultimately suggesting experiments, the instructor exerts a subtle but important control over the discussion. His or her goal is to encourage students to draw upon earlier lectures and exercises, to promote good experimental design, to ensure that all students are vested in the outcome of the experiment, and perhaps most importantly, to steer the discussion toward the preplanned experiment.

Second, the *data collection* phase of the exercise is characterized by collaborative efforts. To establish an information base extensive enough to reveal the desired trends that in turn allow the discovery of a principle, each student must contribute unique data to the class pool. Experiments are often designed so that each student or small groups of students can carry out an individualized modification of the general experimental procedure.

Finally, at a *postlaboratory discovery session* the students examine the pooled data and look for trends. These data and the associated trends are used to answer the prelaboratory questions and, ideally, to support a series of related discoveries. The instructor plays an important role in this aspect of the exercise. Students are introduced to the carefully structured way of thinking and evaluating data that supports scientific creativity. Occasionally, the postlaboratory discussion will call for a short follow-up experimentation session. More often, it will serve as the basis for further presentations in the lecture portion of the course.

Representative Exercise. A description of the discovery exercise "Trends in the Mass of a Collection of Pennies" illustrates many aspects of the program. In addition to introducing students to the scientific method, this laboratory-based exercise exposes them to several important processes and fundamental principles of the discipline.

Consistent with good experimental design, we try to initiate discovery exercises with well-defined questions. Ideally, the question should draw upon prior experiences of the students. The pennies exercise is designed for use early in the first course. Because it is the initial exercise, it is difficult to rely upon a common base of chemical knowledge. Consequently, the focal question for this exercise is the seemingly nonchemical question of what happens to the mass of a penny as the penny ages. All students have the experiential basis to offer an informed hypothesis on the question. Some speculate that the effect of "wear and tear" will cause a penny to lose mass gradually. Others are confident that through corrosion and accumulation of grime a penny gains mass as it ages. Students are prompted to settle the debate by collecting experimental data. They readily devise an appropriate experiment based on measuring the mass of several hundred pennies selected to represent different years of minting. Students are asked to consider the best way to visualize trends in the data. When they decide on a graph of mass as a function of year, they are asked to predict the expected shape of the curve on the basis of whichever hypothesis they favored. This step—relating the possible outcome of the experiment to their predictions—stimulates the students' interest during the subsequent data-collection stage.

At this point all the students have a vested interest in the outcome of the experiment and have thought about how the results might be interpreted. They are ready to enter the laboratory and weigh pennies. Rather than taking enough data to discern the trend, each student weighs ten pennies and contributes these data to an overall class pool. The group data are entered into a computer graphing program and a plot of mass as a function of year of minting is presented on an LCD system and overhead projector.

The trend in mass over time is not clear to each student from the ten points that they individually accumulate. However, a graph of the combined data clearly reveals an unexpected drop in mass in 1982, when zinc replaced copper as the major component in pennies. In addition, for any given year, students observe a considerable range in penny mass. Unexpected results like these stimulate student discussion and sometimes can serve as the focus for further experimentation. In this case, students speculate that the dramatic decrease in mass resulted from either a change in the amount of material used or a change in the composition of the material. Their discussion of how to distinguish between these hypotheses leads to the introduction of the concepts of intensive and extensive properties of matter. In general, one of the students will suggest measuring the intensive property density as a way to check for a change in composition.

After the instructor discusses experimental procedures, the students return to the lab and work cooperatively to obtain mass-volume data. Each student contributes a single point that is used in the preparation of a graph of mass as a function of volume for both old and new pennies. The instructor then discusses extracting information from a graph. The slope, for example, represents the desired density. The concept of relative versus absolute error and the propagation of error through an experiment are also readily illustrated from the data. The difference in slopes (densities) for new and old pennies verifies the hypothesis that the composition of pennies changed in 1982. Students are often interested in returning to the original graph of mass versus year to discuss the causes for the nonuniformity in penny mass for a given year. They identify the inherent uncertainty of a balance, inconsistencies between balances, uneven degree of circulation, differences in location of minting, and the inherent uncertainty in the manufacturing process as worthy of consideration.

Thus, in a single exercise, students experience the process of forming, testing, and refining a hypothesis. They also learn basic techniques of data analysis. Finally, they build an experiential basis for understanding several fundamental concepts.

Observed Benefits of the Discovery Approach

Several benefits of the discovery approach have been observed.

Engaging All Students. In an introductory science curriculum the instructor must accommodate students with very different preparations for the course. If the course is paced for those with a strong high school science background, those with limited or substandard preparation will have trouble competing. In contrast, if the course is geared to the students with a deficient background the better-prepared students may look elsewhere for an intellectual challenge. With an experiment-centered, guided-inquiry approach it is possible to present basic, even routine, material in a way that will make it seem new to all participants. This is illustrated with the exercise "Mass Relationships in Chemical Reactions."

Students completing an introductory chemistry course are generally expected to be able to calculate the mass of product produced in a chemical reaction from a given mass of starting materials. So, for example, a student should be able to calculate the mass of silver chloride produced from 1.0 gram of silver nitrate and an excess of sodium chloride. Usually, the instructor presents a general approach based on converting mass of starting material to amount (in units of moles) followed by application of the balanced chemical equation and finally conversion of the amount of product in moles to the mass of product. Many students have previously worked this type of problem. Although most do not have a complete grasp of what they are doing, some remember the computational algorithm and are able to obtain the right answer.

With the discovery approach, this type of problem can be introduced in a laboratory frame of reference by asking the students to consider an experiment in which a reaction is "calibrated" by running it repeatedly, each time using successively more starting material. Students are asked to predict the shape of a plot of product mass as a function of mass of starting material. They readily predict a linear relationship; the greater the mass of starting material, the greater the mass of product. They also acknowledge that such a graph represents a calibration curve that could be used to predict the mass of product from any mass of starting material. The instructor engages the students in a discussion of how the slope of the calibration curve is related to the nature of the reaction. The exact student response is not crucial. The goal is simply to have students begin to consider that differences in unit masses of products or reactants will contribute to each reaction curve having a unique slope. Their initial predictions about which curves will have the greatest slope are based on a series of reactions proposed by the instructor, which are used to focus their interest on the outcome of the upcoming experimental work. Students are assigned the experimental task of actually preparing calibration curves for the series of reactions discussed during the prelaboratory session. Teams are formed and each is assigned a unique reaction in the series.

At the end of the lab period or during the next lecture, student data are pooled and the instructor leads a discussion of the observed trends. The goal is to have students determine all factors that affect the slope of the calibration curve. The instructor assists by selecting appropriate reactions to compare at each stage. This approach breaks the discovery into a series of manageable insights for individual students. At some point students realize they have developed the ability to predict the slope of any reaction calibration curve without actually doing the experiment. Ultimately, this knowledge is used to develop the traditional computational algorithm for predicting the mass of product from mass of reactant for any chemical reaction.

Although students arrive at the traditional approach to solving routine problems, they may see it in a different light. By building to the approach from experimental data, students have a phenomenological basis for what is too often seen as an abstract series of computations.

One of the most important features of this experiment is that the laboratory frame of reference makes the routine-but-essential material appear new to the well-prepared students without making it too complex for the remaining students. The approach does not necessarily simplify the material presented to students with a weak background in science, but they participate on a more equitable basis. We note that as instructors we pay more attention and respond better to student feedback when a core of students who show an immediate flash of understanding (actually familiarity) for each topic is eliminated. Further, students seem less likely to perceive their struggles as a sign of inferiority in the discipline when none of their classmates has all of the answers.

Encouraging Universal Participation. Laboratory exercises designed to lead students to discoveries are generally more complex than the more traditional verification experiments. Often a single system suffices when the goal is to *verify* a principle previously covered in lecture. However, if the students are to *discover* the principle in the laboratory they usually need to examine a series of systems to establish trends or patterns. A single student or even a pair of students rarely is able to accumulate enough data in a single period to support the discovery process. The experiment must be shared with each student or group of students studying a unique system or performing a variation on an overall theme. Students then pool their results either during or after the laboratory. Although this practice complicates the preparation of an exercise, it encourages even the uncertain student to participate in the postlab session. This phenomenon is illustrated by a discovery exercise that investigates the color of metal complexes.

In this exercise, students are asked to explain why some aqueous solutions of metal ions are colored whereas others are colorless. In the exercise previous to this one, students examine and discuss the hydrogen spectrum. Although this gives them an idea of what causes color in chemical species, they generally decide that they do not have sufficient knowledge about which species are colored to solve the problem. So they decide to collect a data base before beginning an in-depth discussion. Each student takes responsibility for acquiring the spectra of several unique species. In preparation for the group discussion they work out individually the electron configuration of their species. Upon regrouping, students offer and evaluate a number of different hypotheses to explain why only certain members of the series of ions studied are colored. In many cases the hypothesis is consistent with all but one or two of the systems examined. The instructor is aware, from previous experience with the exercise, that the spectra of certain species studied (for example, Ti^{+3}, Zn^{+2}, and Ca^{+2}) will be crucial at specific points in the discussion. Although the color (or lack of it) for each of these species is made available to all students, each student is naturally more familiar and comfortable with his or her own systems. When a new hypothesis is evaluated, students generally examine it first with respect to their specific systems. If the hypothesis is consistent with their systems, they then evaluate it with respect to the larger data pool. This broader consideration is considerably slower as students work through the characteristics of the unfamiliar systems. However, even if a student is less confident or struggling with the process, he or she is clearly the "expert" when one of his or her unique systems is pivotal. This student is then more likely to make a decisive contribution.

Presenting Chemistry as a Way of Knowing. Some students respond to a concept- or task-oriented approach to learning. They accept that specific content and skills from an introductory course will be relevant to a future course or to their career and they respond positively. However, if our pedagogy emphasizes only content we do not serve those students with a holistic or universal approach to education. As they participate in laboratory-based inquiry, these students find relevance in a course that is clearly about more than just facts and theories.

One way to emphasize the universal applicability of the course is to emphasize general processes or strategies. Some of these will be clearly applicable in a variety of fields. For example, we have several exercises that emphasize the use of models and analogies. In one of these exercises students learn basic concepts of metallic and ionic bonding while they simultaneously discover important aspects of how and why familiar macroscopic models can be used to study the microscopic world. The instructor initiates the exercise by suggesting that atoms might be modeled as hard spheres. Students then consider possible ways to arrange atoms in a crystal lattice by thinking about packing a collection of baseballs in a cardboard box. When they find it difficult to describe or characterize possible three-dimensional arrangements, they are introduced to the process of temporarily simplifying a problem by modeling it in two dimensions. Students then generate and evaluate different symmetric patterns of circles on a sheet of paper. They will likely determine that the efficiency of packing can be determined either mathematically with simple geometry or experimentally by cutting out the circles and comparing the mass of the circles to the wasted space. Students tend to discuss whether they need to evaluate the entire sheet of paper or perhaps only a fraction of it. This leads to the idea of finding the smallest representative section of the lattice as a way of simplifying their work.

This insight into the importance of a representative portion (that is, a unit cell) represents one of the central goals of the exercise. Furthermore, when performing the mathematical calculation of the packing efficiency in the unit cell, students see that the radii of the circles cancel from the expression for percentage of wasted space. Usually some students realize that this validates extrapolation of the calculation to circles of any size and perhaps even to the microscopic world of imaginary two-dimensional atoms.

This is only the first section of what can be an extensive introduction to crystal lattices. The relevant aspect to our discussion here is that it illustrates the way the guided inquiry approach focuses instructional time on the general investigative processes while simultaneously introducing important concepts.

General Impressions

We are now in our fifth full year of using laboratory-based, guided-inquiry exercises to drive our general chemistry courses. Eleven different faculty members have participated. Each adapts the approach to fit his or her personal style and preferences. Some focus almost exclusively on the discovery laboratory exercises. Others mix the exercises with a more traditional lecture format. Regardless of the particular emphasis, we find that the approach is seen in a favorable light by students and faculty alike.

Students enjoy doing science in the laboratory and appreciate the sense of camaraderie that comes from the cooperative laboratory efforts and sharing of data. Evidently this approach has had the effect of reducing student stress levels. Our observations in this area were confirmed by the college's director of counseling, who reported a significant decrease over the last five years in the number of students reporting chemistry-course related anxiety.

Before the discovery program, we noted that many students who enjoyed chemistry lectures criticized the laboratory exercises on their course evaluation forms. Consequently we have been particularly impressed by the overwhelmingly positive responses of our students to the laboratory exercises.

Our first two classes of chemistry majors from the discovery curriculum accounted for about 4 percent of the college's graduates in 1993 and 1994. Most of these students elected the major after taking one or more discovery-based courses. Currently, there are 125 chemistry majors at the College of the Holy Cross, representing about 5 percent of the college enrollment. In the spring of 1994, 16 first-year students from the discovery courses added into the chemistry major. During this same period only 1 student dropped the major. Before the new program, additions were usually balanced by withdrawals.

We find that most faculty appreciate the opportunity to focus their teaching efforts on the activity that is at the heart of their discipline. When discussing discovery chemistry, one of our colleagues said that what was initially the most intimidating experience in twenty years of teaching quickly became the most exhilarating. Although much work remains to be done, we have seen occasions when discovery chemistry brings faculty and students together in an environment that generates an excitement for both teaching and learning.

References

Ditzler, M. A., and Ricci, R. W. "Discovery Chemistry: Balancing Structure and Creativity." *Journal of Chemical Education,* 1994, *71,* 685–688.

Jarret, R. M., and McMaster, P. D. "Teaching Organic Chemistry with Student-Generated Information." *Journal of Chemical Education,* in press.

Ricci, R. W., and Ditzler, M. A. "Discovery Chemistry: A Laboratory-Centered Approach to Teaching General Chemistry." *Journal of Chemical Education,* 1991, *68,* 228.

MAURI A. DITZLER was chair and professor of chemistry at the College of the Holy Cross in Worcester, Massachusetts, when the curriculum described in this report was developed and implemented. He is now dean of arts and sciences and professor of chemistry at Millikin University in Decatur, Illinois.

ROBERT W. RICCI is professor of chemistry at the College of the Holy Cross where he has been actively involved in developing discovery chemistry for the past five years. Currently he is exploring ways of extending the program into the arts and social sciences.

Faculty at the Colorado School of Mines have developed a program that introduces freshman and sophomore engineering and science students to open-ended problem solving, to teamwork, and to communication.

Real-World Problem Solving in Freshman-Sophomore Engineering

Michael J. Pavelich, Barbara M. Olds, Ronald L. Miller

Develop an efficient, nonintrusive mechanism for loading a wheelchair onto a bus in less than thirty seconds. Design software that will perform mass balance calculations. Perform an energy audit for Denver, Colorado, to determine if the mandated oxygenated fuels program is effective. Develop fire safety standards for mountain communities where the risk of wildfire is extremely high.

These and hundreds of other projects for customers in industry and government have been undertaken over the past decade by Colorado School of Mines (CSM) students—students who are freshmen and sophomores in the award-winning EPICS program.

EPICS (Engineering Practices Introductory Course Sequence) was developed to help students at CSM learn and practice open-ended problem solving, teamwork, and communication during their first four semesters in college. In their EPICS classes, students work in teams to solve increasingly complex problems for clients from industry and government and to report their results to a variety of audiences (Olds, Pavelich, and Yeatts, 1990). This hands-on approach introduces our science and engineering students at the beginning of their college careers to the kinds of problem-solving abilities they will need as professionals. We have gathered considerable evidence, both qualitative and quantitative, to support our approach. In addition, we have some evidence that project-focused classes involving teamwork and hands-on experiences may be particularly appealing to women students because they provide an active, "warm" climate in which to learn. In this chapter we will briefly discuss the CSM context, describe the EPICS program, and present the results of our evaluation efforts to date.

The Colorado School of Mines

The Colorado School of Mines is a small, selective school of engineering and applied science concentrating on the minerals and resource industries. Our student body, of approximately two thousand undergraduates and eight hundred graduate students, comes from all fifty states as well as a number of foreign countries. Approximately 22 percent of the 1992 entering freshman class were women, 10 percent were ethnic minorities—mainly Latinos, African Americans, Asian Americans, and Native Americans—and 14 percent were foreign students.

CSM has a long history of responding to societal and industry demands. In 1979 we surveyed alumni, faculty, students, employers, and industry leaders about the qualities they thought engineers of the future should possess. The resulting document, *Profile of the Future Graduate* (Bull, 1979), outlined six major attributes: technical competence, lifelong learning, communication and teamwork, breadth of interest, self-education, and integrity and self-discipline.

This profile marked a departure for CSM, which, like most engineering schools, had focused primarily on graduating students with unquestioned technical skills. Our faculty responded to the challenge of educating our students to develop the other attributes as well and, as one result, the EPICS program was started in 1981.

The EPICS Program

Faculty concern about the limited opportunities for lower-division undergraduates to solve realistic open-ended problems prompted an interdisciplinary group of faculty to develop a series of four courses that emphasized real-world problem-solving, team-building, and oral and written technical communication skills. With support from the Exxon Education Foundation, the pilot EPICS courses were taught in 1981 to a small group of volunteer students. In 1984 the program was approved by the faculty and became a requirement for all freshmen and sophomores. As EPICS was developed and refined, we made use of current research in areas such as personality type and learning styles (for example, the Myers-Briggs Type Indicator [Myers, 1987; McCaulley, 1990] and Kolb's model of experiential learning [Kolb, 1984; Terry, Durrant, Hurt, and Williamson, 1991]). In 1986 and again in 1988 EPICS was named a Program of Excellence by the Colorado Commission on Higher Education.

EPICS Projects

One of the most innovative aspects of the program is the project/communications (P/C) portion of each of the four EPICS courses. In this portion, students solve problems in teams and communicate results to both clients and professors. Each P/C experience is designed to build upon previous project work and to improve the problem-solving, team, and communication skills of each student. The specific emphases of each P/C course are as follows:

Team-based, open-ended problem solving, team building, and written technical communication skills (first semester)
Information-literacy, self-education, and oral technical communication skills (second semester)
Application of engineering analysis, synthesis, and evaluation to open-ended problem solving (third semester)
Professional client relations and appreciation for client's culture and values (fourth semester).

All EPICS P/C sections are team-taught by an engineer or scientist and a communication specialist. Their role is to coach or manage the student design teams, rather than to lecture to students. Faculty serve as resources—teachers of both content and process—and as liaisons between clients and students. Classes meet once or twice a week in two-hour blocks with no more than thirty minutes devoted to minilectures, announcements of upcoming deadlines, and general feedback about progress on the project. Students work in permanent design teams throughout the semester; all assignments are directed toward satisfactory completion of the project and professional presentation of their results and recommendations to their client.

A Freshman Project: Remediation of Mine Drainage Contamination. As a first example, we will describe the project/communications portion of the second course in the EPICS sequence. Students entering this class have completed one semester of team-based project work in which they participated in team-building exercises, received instruction in technical writing and report preparation, and completed their first open-ended project. In this semester we emphasize instruction and practice in professional oral communication. Students also continue to practice problem solving, team building skills, and written technical communication skills while working on a new semesterlong, open-ended project for an industrial or governmental client.

Problem Definition. During the first week of class, student design teams receive a letter from their client describing in general terms the open-ended problem they must solve. Recently, for example, the Colorado Division of Natural Resources asked students to develop remediation plans for several mine drainage contamination sites in Clear Creek County, Colorado. To understand the project, teams first identified and defined key words in the client letter; later they presented oral and written clarifications of their problem definition for client approval.

Area Study. To reinforce the idea that not all knowledge is gained from instructors or textbooks and to help students become "information literate," much of the first half of the semester is spent acquiring background information relevant to the project. Each student becomes the team's "expert" in a specific area; experts from different teams exchange information, reinforcing the idea that peers are valid sources of knowledge. To complete successfully the mine drainage remediation project, student experts learned about regulatory requirements, groundwater hydrology, economics, slope stability, and aqueous chemistry. Students also visited the remediation sites, interviewed interested parties including landowners and county officials, and met several times with their client during the semester. At midterm, each study group produced a written report and delivered an oral presentation of its findings to the project teams.

Problem Solution and Client Recommendations. To develop solutions and recommendations, the students brainstorm to find alternative solutions, consider applicable constraints and assumptions, study information gathered in the study groups, and build consensus. They also defend their team's proposed solution in a cross-examination and finally present the results of their work to their client both orally and in writing. For the remediation project, representatives of the Colorado Department of Natural Resources attended student presentations and received a rich and well-developed collection of proposed remediation strategies for mine contamination sites. These results were subsequently used by the client to prepare a formal remediation plan for the state of Colorado.

A Sophomore Project Course: Creating Computer Software. Sophomores complete more sophisticated projects stressing engineering analysis, synthesis, and evaluation. The primary purpose of the first sophomore-level course is to give students a working command of a high-level computer language using a project in which students design, create, test, and deliver a computer software package that meets a client's needs. The study of programming and project work run in parallel throughout the semester. For the first two-thirds of the semester, most of the class time is spent on traditional learning of the computer language; however, for the last third of the semester nearly all class and laboratory time is devoted to completion of the project.

Problem Definition. While learning the programming language, students become familiar with their client's needs and project objectives, learn the technical details of the project, and design (but do not code) their program using flowcharts and structure charts. For example, students developed a quantitative analysis tutor for two professors in CSM's chemistry department. The clients wanted a software program that would check students' calculations in an analytical laboratory course without giving the correct answers. The students' primary challenge was to develop a user-friendly program into which a user could easily input and correct a five-by-ten matrix of data. Ideas for the software were presented to the clients as a written proposal and program plan.

Analysis and Synthesis. Once the students have become familiar with the programming language and have completed their program designs, each design team begins to code individual subprograms that are eventually combined to form a final executable software product. Every student is required to write and debug at least one significant subprogram for his or her team; students quickly discover the need to share detailed information among their teammates to ensure that subprograms can "talk" to the rest of the code as planned. In the quantitative analysis project, typical programs were two thousand lines long. As coding proceeds, students also begin to design and write their program user's manual by documenting their programming work and deciding how best to help a user work with the new software.

Software Evaluation. During the final weeks of the semester, teams intensify the evaluation of their software using feedback from the course instructors and teammates. A continual cycle of modification and reevaluation occurs until students demonstrate the "final" version of the software for their client at the end of the semester. The team also submits a final working program and user manual to the course instructors for grading. Over twenty teams worked on the quantitative analysis tutor and all submitted successful final programs that met the clients' basic needs. The best program has been used, without alteration, for the past three semesters in the analytical chemistry laboratory course.

Program Evaluation

In its early years, verbal feedback every two weeks from students in the pilot program was used to alter the courses on the fly. Subsequently, we have collected a variety of evaluation data on the effectiveness of EPICS.

Participant Response. Anecdotal evidence on the value of putting students in project teams to work on real-world problems is extremely favorable. Student and faculty feedback indicate that many students experience a great deal of frustration in their first or second project but resolve those feelings and noticeably improve their skills from project to project. Thus, the projects are definitely the learning experience they were intended to be.

The following are some typical quotes from graduating seniors: "All real problems in engineering are open ended. I feel confident I can handle them, and I look forward to doing that," and "The projects gave me a good feeling for how my profession works and how to work with other people." Comments from professors like this one are similarly typical: "This team (EP 202) struggled with each other and the project all semester. But they put together a final oral presentation that knocked the socks off the clients (a city council). They really put it all together, very impressive thinking and communicating." Project clients also consistently have high praise for the results of project work. Typical quotes are the following: "The students did an excellent job of taking a somewhat vague assignment and defining a final product that will be useful to us," and "We were impressed with the students' ability to tackle the technical aspects, but also their ability to divvy up the problem and to make a presentation that was appropriate for our audience."

Although we did not design the EPICS program to address specifically concerns of women students, it appears that the project work may be of particular benefit to them. We recently interviewed fourteen women students about their perceptions of studying engineering and science, and asked their opinion on working in project teams. A majority of the group, which consisted of freshmen, juniors, and seniors, said that working in project teams was a comfortable and effective way for them to learn. They cited sharing ideas with others and having professors out of the lecture mode as distinct advantages. Many also cited as an advantage the fact that the projects modeled how their professions operate.

Intellectual Development Measured with the Perry Model. As an additional measure of the effect of our curricula, we are collecting data using William G. Perry's model of intellectual development (Perry, 1968). The results, presented in this section, indicate that substantial intellectual growth occurs in our students but also that refinement of our program is probably warranted.

Perry observed patterns in how students perceive knowledge and value, patterns that are hierarchical and chronological and thus describe a developmental process. Perceptions vary from a dualistic view (where all ideas are perceived as right or wrong or black or white) to a relativistic view (where determining "right" requires a complex, contextual judgment). Perry translated these patterns into a nine-position model of development (see Perry, 1968, or the articles referenced in Pavelich and Moore, 1993). To illustrate Perry's model, positions 2, 4, and 6 are briefly sketched in this section with examples of behavior observed in students working on open-ended projects in the EPICS program.

Students at position 2 are dualists. They see the world in a bifurcated fashion: right versus wrong, good versus bad. All right is determined by the authority figure. There is no need for evidence in an argument; one needs only to quote the authority's "right" answer. In fact, the use of evidence is not understood. The plurality of views that exist in the world and the uncertainty inherent in some knowledge are acknowledged by the student but are seen as shortcomings in the authority. Freshman students working on an open-ended project exhibit position 2 thinking when they are appalled to find that neither the client nor the professor has a definite answer to the problem.

Students who have evolved to position 4 accept uncertainty as legitimate and something to expect, but they are still uncomfortable with it. They become more skilled in the use of evidence, but the activity is often seen as "how authority wants us to think" rather than as a consequence of the nature of knowledge. Yet position 4 students can be very suspicious of the truth of any evidence. Many feel that "everyone's opinion is equally valid." Because all opinions are equal, commitment to decisions is very low. Position 4 behavior is exhibited in project teams that develop solid arguments for one solution and see no advantage in exploring alternative solutions.

A student capable of position 6 thinking is a competent open-ended problem solver. Using evidence, evaluating alternatives, and making contextual judgments are now seen as the natural and necessary approaches to our world. The uncertainty of data and the spectrum of human values that were seen as disconnected aberrations (labeled multiplicity) are seen as the connected, inherent nature of things (labeled relativism). At position 6 the student also begins to see the need for commitment as a logical response to the uncertainty of our knowledge. Commitment is defined as taking positive action, based on reason and personal standards, within the context of the situation considered.

This model gives EPICS instructors a construct to understand some students' reactions to project work and has helped ease the frustrations of teaching and learning in this mode. Moreover, because the model speaks directly to the perspective an individual uses to solve real-world, open-ended problems, we judged it to be a good measure of how well our program prepares students to operate as effective professionals. Our working hypothesis is that the four years of undergraduate education should move students from positions 2–3 to positions 5–6. Position 6 is a satisfactory description of a professional problem solver.

Over the last three years, we have collected data on our entering freshmen, second-semester sophomores, and graduating seniors using measures based on Perry's model. We use hourlong structured interviews of individual students that are videotaped and then viewed by Perry rating experts (Pavelich and Moore, 1993). To date, we have interviewed forty-five freshmen, thirty-four sophomores, and thirty seniors. The freshman-versus-senior data are presented in Figure 5.1. We will be collecting more data, especially on seniors. However, the collected data do allow analysis.

Figure 5.1. CSM Freshmen Versus Seniors

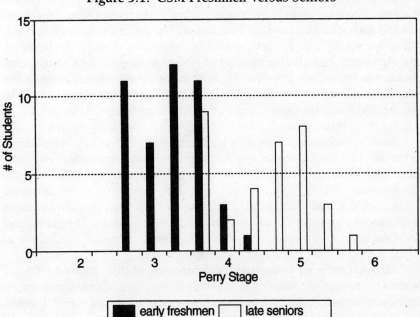

The average Perry position for each population in our data is the following: freshmen, 3.3; sophomores, near 3.7; seniors, near 4.5. Thus there is a statistically significant linear increase during the undergraduate years. The distribution curves give us richer information. From Figure 5.1 we see that no freshman in our sample is a true dualist (positions 1.0 to 2.0); most are at position 3.0 or above. However, only a very small number are at position 4. No seniors have remained at position 3.0; most are above 4.0. More than a third of seniors have reached position 5.0, but none measured at 6.0.

Viewing the interviews, we developed a deep pride in the maturity of thought and the excitement and commitment most seniors express. If anything, the Perry scale is conservative in recognizing this development. Yet the data show a slower development than we would like. Most telling is that more than half the seniors have not even reached position 5. As a result, CSM faculty are discussing, designing, and testing new emphases in our teaching that may accelerate our students' development; the current Perry data will serve as a baseline against which any changes in EPICS and other programs can be evaluated.

Measurement of Written and Oral Communication Skills. An advantage of using real-world projects is that they allow the students to learn and practice communication skills in a context that closely resembles professional activity, spurring the development of such skills (Olds, 1987). That we have achieved this advantage is clear from several sources. The first is our state-mandated schoolwide assessment data base. CSM uses portfolios of student work to monitor their learning. To monitor communication skills we collect project reports, term papers, and videotapes of oral presentations on a sampling of our students. These are periodically studied by groups of faculty from across campus and each student's progress is evaluated. The pattern seen in these evaluations is a strong improvement in abilities, especially through the freshmen and sophomore years. In the summer of 1992 the assessment committee concluded that the average first-semester freshman scored 2.9 in organization (on a scale where 1 equaled no mastery and 5 equaled complete mastery) whereas the average second-semester sophomore, completing EPICS, scored 3.6; in content, the averages were 2.8 for freshmen and 3.5 for sophomores.

A second source of information is the companies that recruit our students. In the late 1970s recruiters told us that the communication skills of our graduates were generally weak. As noted earlier, this type of feedback led to the development of EPICS. In 1991, a curriculum committee again canvassed companies that hire our alumni. This time the response on communication skills was very positive. Of the nearly two hundred responses, 25 percent rated CSM students' communication skills as "strong"; over half rated them as "adequate"; and only 15 percent rated them as "weak."

Measurement of Computer Programming Skills. Before EPICS, 25 percent or more of the students in our introductory programming course generally were unsuccessful; that is, they dropped out or earned a D or F grade.

The same course taught using an open-ended project saw the failure rate drop to near 10 percent (Miller, Buzbee, Pavelich, and Olds, 1992). This is not a result of the grading process because, to pass, each student must earn a C or better on programming exams that have not changed in difficulty over the years. The success rate of females is slightly higher than that of males in both class modes. More striking is that both groups of students show a dramatic increase in success rate (or drop in failure rate) when the course is restructured using an open-ended team project. We have also found that the attitude of students toward the programming course and their confidence in working with computers rose noticeably as measured through student course evaluations.

Conclusion

The EPICS program demonstrates that the learning of traditional content material is enhanced when students deal with that content in the context of an open-ended, "real-life" project. Learning in this way increases student interest, probably by facilitating cross-content associations created naturally in their minds. Centering on a project also opens more avenues of learning for the student. Kolb's learning style theory, for example, recognizes that there are many ways to learn. One key reason for our students' success may be that our program offers several avenues for learning. In the project-centered classes we have coupled typical lecture learning with team-based learning and open-ended exploration of issues. Perhaps most striking about our experiences, however, is that we have conclusive evidence that open-ended problem-solving abilities can be effectively enhanced at the freshman and sophomore levels.

References

Bull, R. (ed.). *Profile of the Future Graduate.* Colorado School of Mines, Golden, 1979.

Kolb, D. A. *Experiential Learning: Experience as the Source of Learning and Development.* Englewood Cliffs, N.J.: Prentice Hall, 1984.

McCaulley, M. H. "The MBTI and Individual Pathways in Engineering Design." *Engineering Education,* 1990, *80* (5), 537–542.

Miller, R. L., Buzbee, G. A., Pavelich, M. J., and Olds, B. M. "A New Pedagogical Approach to Computer Programming and Problem Solving in the Engineering Classroom." In *Proceedings of the Frontiers in Education Conference,* New York, 1992.

Myers, I. B. *Introduction to Type.* (4th ed.) Palo Alto, Calif.: Consulting Psychologists Press, 1987.

Olds, B. M. "Beyond the Casebook: Teaching Technical Communication Through 'Real Life' Projects." *The Technical Writing Teacher,* Jan. 1987, pp. 11–17.

Olds, B. M., Pavelich, M. J., and Yeatts, F. R. "Teaching the Design Process to Freshmen and Sophomores." *Engineering Education,* July/Aug. 1990, pp. 554–559.

Pavelich, M. J., and Moore, W. S. "Measuring Maturation Rates of Engineering Students Using the Perry Model." In *Proceedings of the 1993 Frontiers in Education Conference,* New York, 1993.

Perry, W. G. *Forms of Intellectual and Ethical Development in the College Years.* Troy, Mo.: Holt, Rinehart & Winston, 1968.

Terry, R. E., Durrant, S. O., Hurt, P. K., and Williamson, K. J. "Implementation of the Kolb Learning Style Theory in a Faculty Development Program at Brigham Young University." In *Proceedings of the 1991 ASEE Conference,* Washington, D.C., 1991.

MICHAEL J. PAVELICH *is professor of chemistry and director of the Office of Teaching Effectiveness at the Colorado School of Mines.*

BARBARA M. OLDS *is director of the McBride Honors Program and associate professor of liberal arts and international studies at the Colorado School of Mines.*

RONALD L. MILLER *is director of EPICS and associate professor of chemical engineering and petroleum refining at the Colorado School of Mines.*

This chapter presents an overview of the first course in computer science offered at City College of New York. The course is a strong departure from conventional introductory programming courses, offering students a logic-based introduction to program design.

Formal Methods, Design, and Collaborative Learning in the First Computer Science Course

Douglas R. Troeger

The conventional first course in computer science does not work very well.

• As evidenced by many dozens of beginning programming texts, the course all too often degenerates into a syntax lesson, teaching little more than the features of some particular computer language.

• Despite lip service, there is no satisfactory design methodology. Students write programs by trial and error, mimicking programs they have seen in the text and learned about in lectures. When their code works on the few test cases provided by the instructor, they turn it in and pray. It may or may not be correct, and in either case they are usually at a loss to explain why.

Usually, the best students are bored in these courses ("Is this all there is to computer science?"). The others, for whom the programming process is as mysterious at term's end as it was at the beginning, are left wondering what they missed.

We believe it is possible to do much better. The first course in computer science (CSc 102) at City College of New York (CCNY) was restructured in

I am grateful for the advice and encouragement of Professor Daniel D. McCracken of City College in the development and implementation of the course described in this chapter. I am grateful as well to Dean Charles B. Watkins of the School of Engineering of City College for suggesting that I consider using the Treisman model in CSc 102. Finally, I am glad to acknowledge the support of the National Science Foundation (CDA–9114481) in funding both the development and implementation of CSc 102 and the support of the City University of New York in funding Project ACCESS.

1990 as an introduction to problem solving and programming based on principles of program verification developed by pioneers in computing science (Floyd, 1967; Hoare, 1969; Dijkstra, 1976). The main goals of the new course are to develop students' skill in designing programs and to equip students with logical tools, enabling them to explain how and why their programs work. The course seeks to empower students reliably to design, refine, and certify their programs by drawing their attention to the details of the logic underlying the programming process. Our experience has found the following:

Beginning students can master a formal problem-solving methodology that is at once powerful and practical.

Although the coverage of the syntax of the course language (Pascal) has been reduced, students' ability to use what they were taught to design programs dramatically exceeds that achieved by our students exposed to more standard courses.

Students who learn the style of program development presented in the course are able to explain how and why their programs work.

We have found too that the immediacy of the application (that is, to develop a working program) piques student interest in logic and proofs, and that the course serves as an applied introduction to logic as well.

Logic as the Organizing Concept in the First Course

What is the role of logic in teaching programming? Students realize very quickly that the conceptual gap between problem statement, or specification, and its algorithmic solution is frequently large. Consider, for example, the problem of computing the greatest common divisor (*gcd*) of two positive integers. On the one hand, we have the simple specification: for input consisting of the positive integers x and y, the output is to be the *gcd* of x and y. On the other hand, we have the following sequence of steps, or algorithm, for finding greatest common divisors (this is Euclid's algorithm):

Step 1: Initialize m to x, and n to y.
Step 2: If $m = n$, return m as the answer and stop. Otherwise continue to Step 3.
Step 3: If $m > n$, then replace m by $m - n$ and go to Step 2. Otherwise, replace n by $n - m$ and go to Step 2.

What is the connection between these? Given only this sequence of steps, would your beginning students recognize their purpose? Stated more generally, the question is, how does one make the transition from an algorithm, or its expression as a program, to an understanding of what it does? Conversely, given a specification, how does one find a program that realizes that specification? For students, these questions represent the most difficult aspect of programming. *The role of logic in teaching programming is to help students successfully navigate the passage between a problem's statement and its algorithmic solution.*

Using Logic to Understand What an Algorithm Does. To make the point that logic is both a powerful and accessible tool for students as they seek to understand algorithms, we outline an argument showing that Euclid's algorithm behaves as claimed. We show that for positive input integers x and y, the algorithm yields as output the greatest common divisor of x and y. Put another way, we demonstrate the *correctness* of Euclid's algorithm.

For any valid input, the algorithm's execution will follow a similar pattern. After Step 1, there will be some number (perhaps zero) of executions of the sequence <Step 2; Step 3>. If the algorithm ever terminates, Step 2 will be the last step. With this information, we can proceed as follows. First, we observe (*) that after each execution of Step 3 it is true that $gcd(m,n)$ is equal to $gcd(x,y)$, the greatest common divisor of the input values, x and y. This follows from the mathematical facts (i) $gcd(m,n) = gcd(m - n, n)$, and (ii) $gcd(m,n) = gcd(m, n - m)$. Next, we note that m and n are initially positive, and that if m and n are positive prior to any execution of Step 3, they remain positive after the execution of Step 3. Finally, we see (**) that any execution on valid input must eventually reach Step 2 with $m = n$. Since one can subtract positive (integer) amounts from a positive integer only finitely many times before one obtains a negative result, it must be the case that any execution requires only finitely many applications of Step 3. It follows finally from (*) and (**), and the fact that $gcd(m,m) = m$ for any positive integer m, that any execution on valid input x, y must eventually output $gcd(x,y)$.

What do we learn from this argument? As students, we appreciate the fact that it lays the algorithm bare: nothing of the algorithm's correctness or of its limitations (what if $x < 0$?) remains a mystery. We feel that every nut and bolt of the algorithm has been made available for our inspection. The contrast to the limited insight obtained from trying test cases, even while carefully and methodically tracing the execution of the algorithm, is striking. As teachers, we are excited by the prospects of being able actually *to explain* our designs. We note that the argument, even when fleshed out with the missing details [beginning students generally do not know, for example, that $gcd(m,n) = gcd(m - n, n)$], is not long. Moreover, although it is not trivial, it is also not sophisticated: the argument is based on nothing more than an understanding of the sequencing of the algorithm's steps, a few facts from the problem domain, some elementary propositional logic, and induction. All of these concepts are readily accessible to beginning students.

Using Logic to Develop Programs. More important than retrofitting an explanation to an existing algorithm, however, is the discovery of algorithms in the first place. How can we help students use logic to develop insight and experience in coming up with good designs?

To a beginner, programming might be succinctly characterized as a process of moving back and forth between specification and code. Working from the specification, one makes a first guess at an algorithm for achieving the transition from *precondition* (the requirements imposed by the specification on the program's input) to *postcondition* (the requirements imposed by the specification on the program's output). Next, perhaps using the computer to test the algorithm, one checks to see whether it does what it was hoped to do, and refines accordingly, iterating the process again. But how does one prevent this from degenerating to a frequently endless and frustrating process of trial and error, a cycle of "guess, test, guess again, test again"?

This is precisely the role of logic. Very early in the course, we offer students the following advice: *The meanings of a program's variables ought to be precisely defined, and these meanings ought to be held invariant throughout the program.* These definitions arise in the course of developing a basic approach, a *design idea,* for the program, and are then kept at the front of one's mind during the process of moving back and forth between specification and code. Logic provides answers to the questions: (i) Are my definitions really as useful as I thought? (ii) What must the program do next to keep my definitions true? and (iii) Does my program maintain its variables' definitions?

We illustrate the approach by beginning the development of a program to compute factorials. We begin the design process by considering the structure of the problem, seeking a design idea. In the present case, we can use the definition: $0! = 1$, and for $m \geq 1$, $m! = m \times (m - 1)!$ This implies that if we have stored the value $(m - 1)!$ in some variable *fact,* then we can set fact to $m!$ simply by multiplying it by m. Thus, to compute the factorial of $n \geq 1$, all we need do is to multiply some variable fact initialized to 1 by the integers 1, 2,$^{\circ}$, n, in turn. To implement the sequence of multiplications, we use another variable, *count,* which will count from 0 up to n; we envision the final program as a *while* loop, with driving condition *count* <> n (read "*count* not equal to n").

At this point, students would traditionally begin coding their solution, relying on trial and error to work out the remaining details. (How, for example, should *count* be initialized? Should *count* be incremented before or after it has been used to update fact in the *while* loop? What if $n = 0$?)

In contrast, we ask students to answer the following question before beginning coding: what definitions, or design roles, ought the variables *count* and *fact* satisfy? Design roles set out, as precisely as we can at a given stage in the program's development, our notions of variables' meaning. In the present case, we intend that (1) *fact* is equal to the factorial of the current value of *count,* that is, that *fact* = *count*! and (2) *count* equals the number of multiplications that have occurred so far. The usefulness of these definitions is evident: if we can write a *while* loop that keeps these true, using *count* <> n as the *while* driver, then on termination of that loop we will have *count* = n and hence *fact* = $n!$.

Thus the overall problem ("Write a program to compute factorials") has been reduced to the smaller problems of first achieving, and then maintaining, the validity of these design roles while making progress toward termination.

Let us indicate briefly how these tasks can be accomplished, focusing first on maintaining the validity of the definitions. Assuming that the design roles are satisfied before some execution of the loop body, what actions must the loop body carry out to ensure that the design roles hold afterwards? In accordance with our design idea, we replace *count* by *count* + 1. Since *fact* = *count*! before we increased *count*, we now have *fact* = (*count* − 1)!. So we need only multiply *fact* by *count* to regain the design roles. Thus our loop is given as follows:

```
while count <> n do
begin
count := count + 1;
fact := count * fact
end;
```

(Reversing the order of the assignments within the *while* loop, however, yields a program which does not preserve the design role of *fact*.) The choice of initial values for *count* and *fact* is equally straightforward: by its definition, *count* must be 0 before any multiplications have occurred, and, correspondingly, *fact* must be 1.

We emphasize that although this example would be presented quite early in the course (in the fourth week), the approach it embodies generalizes readily to more complex programs.

Course Delivery

A key feature of the course, in addition to its novel presentation of programming, is its delivery. Students are grouped into teams of two or three, and the class is organized as a group of collaborative learning communities, on lines suggested by Treisman (1985). Each team is joined by a peer tutor, an undergraduate who has successfully completed the course. Each team is asked to complete one program and its documentation every week once the three-week introductory phase of the course has been completed. In this course, a program's documentation includes a careful justification of the program's correctness. For the first third of the term, class time is split between lecture and the departmental Macintosh laboratory. Later, it is split between lecture and smaller recitation classes. Collaborative work occurs on the students' time, in a small Macintosh-equipped lab set aside expressly for this purpose. Student teams are expected to meet with their peer tutors at least one hour each week. In practice, most teams meet considerably more frequently, especially after midterm. We adhere to our schedule of weekly programming assignments even as the problems become more difficult.

The peer tutors are themselves coached and assisted by graduate mentors who are doctoral students in computer science or computer engineering and have themselves been thoroughly instructed in the course techniques.

The tutors and mentors play an important role in the course. In addition to facilitating directly student learning of the new material, they steer the less prepared students to additional tutoring (usually in basic math) that is available on the City College campus. They also provide an additional feedback loop to the course instructor, modulating the pace and content of the lectures. The effectiveness of the tutoring is maintained by arranging to have the mentors meet regularly with the course instructor; at the very least, the instructor needs to discuss approaches and solutions to the current homework problem.

The attitude of the staff toward the course is this: "We are there to facilitate students' learning, and we do not view the course in any way as a 'filter.' One consequence is that we are very free with hints during the group working sessions, although we do not permit students to take notes while we are giving out these hints. Students can ask all the (reasonable) questions they like, and we attempt to give them straight answers—but we insist that they seek understanding while working with us, and then go away and try to write down what they have understood. If they get stuck doing so, we're always available for another round of questions."

Throughout the course we stress professionalism and social responsibility: programs are increasingly important and increasingly complex and their correctness increasingly crucial. Some rigorous development process is necessary if reliability is to be attained. It is somewhat shocking to most people to realize that, to date, most software has been produced without the benefit of even the formality implicit in the construction engineer's blueprint, and that virtually all existing software is riddled with bugs. Students must grasp the consequences of the fact that, in more than a few applications, health and safety rely on the correctness of programs.

Guiding Principles

Summarized in this section are several guiding principles that have proved instrumental in presenting this material to beginning students. We have grouped these into two broad categories: principles to be enacted by the instructor and principles that we encourage students to adopt.

Principles for the Instructor. The instructor's main task is to orchestrate the simultaneous presentation of logic and programming.

Provide Essential Background Knowledge. The first three weeks of the semester are given over to essential introductory topics, specifically: (1) a brief and elementary discussion of what it means to solve problems with the help of a computer; (2) basic machine concepts; (3) a detailed presentation of the syntax and operational semantics of a subset of the Pascal language, including just Boolean and integer variables, assignment, sequencing, *if-then-else, while, read,* and *write;* and (4) an introductory treatment of some basic concepts in logic, namely the Boolean connectives, necessity, sufficiency, and a few examples of arguments by induction. All of these logical concepts arise naturally in discussing the syntax rules of the Pascal subset.

Focus on Very Simple Programs at First. In our experience, this restriction allows students the time to become accustomed to the very idea of using a design methodology in their programming. We arrange our presentation so that design problems considered first in the course all yield to *while* programs whose loop bodies consist entirely of sequenced assignment statements: no *ifs*, no nested *whiles*, and so on. It achieves this by limiting the scope and number of choices students need to make. We restrict ourselves early on as well to programs whose variables' design roles are logical conjunctions of simple conditions.

In addition, our early examples tend to be based on elementary pre-calculus mathematics. We seek not to distract students from our presentation of the methodology in the first part of the term. In our experience, this is best achieved by sticking to problems with unambiguous, simple specifications. Nonetheless, we take pains to keep the course from feeling like a mathematics class: even though the early programming problems are drawn mostly from the common intersection of students' math backgrounds, we focus on the programming process rather than on what these problems teach us about mathematics.

Present Logic Only as It Is Needed. It is worth emphasizing as well that we essentially never isolate the logic introduced in the course from its application to programming. We don't, for example, ask students to solve the usual induction exercises ("Show that the sum of the first n odd numbers is n^2"), though these ideas do frequently turn up in the guise of programming exercises ("Write a program to compute n^2 using the following method"); similarly, we never quiz or examine students on the usual word problems of elementary logic. We use the associated concepts, again and again. Students see these basic concepts first in simple form, later in a deeper form. Eventually the student has seen a topic enough times, from sufficiently many perspectives, to understand it thoroughly. The general concept of induction, for example (on which our correctness arguments are based), is introduced only after students have already agreed that the strategy, seen in several examples, is a reasonable one. Even for evaluation purposes, students' understanding of these ideas is checked only in the context of programming. This approach has had the effect of "removing the sting" from material that, presented alone (the dreaded mathematical intermezzo), strikes many students as both forbidding and unmotivated. It permits students to master the use of a few important mathematical tools in a setting that matters to them; based on anecdotal evidence, at least, it also seems to leave many students with a taste for more. *The logic needed throughout the course is presented on a just-in-time basis, and then we present only precisely as much as is needed.*

Introduce More Advanced Programming Features in Accordance with the Complexity of Their Associated Logic. Arrays, for example, require a brief introduction to dummy variables and (what amounts to) finite quantification; procedures call for a somewhat deeper (but still informal) look at variable bindings. As the term progresses, students' ability to deal with such concepts increases, but one must be sensitive to the fact that students have not had a prior course in logic. Each new programming construct introduced requires discussion of its associated logic. Indeed, we seek to convey the idea that one ought never program with a particular language feature until its logic has been thoroughly understood.

Choose Programming Problems to Foreshadow Future Study in Computer Science. To counteract the tight focus of the initial part of the course on programming methodology, problems in the second part of the course are selected to give students a glimpse of computer science as much as to allow them to hone their programming skills. Typical projects immediately following the midterm involve searching, sorting, combinatorics, and two or three larger assignments emphasizing top-down design. These latter problems are ambitious, but not overly so.

Principles for the Students. The student's main task is to learn to view the logic as an aid, and not as a hindrance, to programming.

Develop Design Roles Before Programming. We expend a great deal of effort to bring students to the point where they are willing to work out their variables' design roles before they code their first guess at a solution. Students tend to want to produce code as soon as possible, no doubt because they are more comfortable fiddling with that code (treating the problem as some kind of crossword puzzle) than working at the more abstract level needed to discover and verify design roles.

This problem is particularly acute for students who have been previously exposed to programming. They have been taught that programs work by changing variables' values, so what point can there be in focusing on anything other than the sequences of values which a program's variables assume during execution? Why focus on these stationary definitions rather than on the dynamic history of the variables' value sequences?

Early in the course, we overcome this problem by keeping students' attention focused on the methodology rather than on the programs themselves; later, as more complex problems are tackled, we make every effort to convince students of the many engineering benefits of deferring coding until after the design roles have been thought out.

We ask students to adopt the following working style: do not go anywhere near a computer for at least the first hour devoted to a programming assignment (perhaps the first two hours, later in the term). The design idea, the variables' design roles, and the initial refinements ought to be checked first using paper and pencil. There is really nothing a student can do with a computer that will help with the initial design.

Test Programs Logically. People who are unfamiliar with this approach are frequently surprised by how much work there is to do before going to the computer, but we do not want to leave the impression that it is never appropriate to set fingers to keys. Once a design has been developed to the point achieved in the factional example, in fact, it makes a great deal of sense to enter and test it. In spite of the best intentions, a design methodology is still vulnerable to errors, and difficulties encountered at this point may well force one to rethink basic aspects of one's design.

Thus testing remains important. Though testing cannot (in principle) reveal the absence of errors, it can surely be of assistance in revealing their presence. How should one advise students to go about testing a program?

Should one, as is frequently done, randomly choose input values and then check that the program gives the right output for each? Certainly it is possible to discover design flaws in this manner, but a better method is available. Students can exploit variables' design roles in testing as well as in development. The basic idea is simple: we want to examine variable values as the program runs and check that these values conform to the intended design roles. One either uses a debugger to accomplish this or resorts to the time-honored technique of inserting *write* statements at strategic points in the program.

Consider Alternative Designs. One of the main advantages of this approach is the ease with which it allows comparison and contrast of alternate designs. Continuing a bit further with our factorial program, we can, for example, consider the possibility of running *count* from n down to 0. In this case the design role of *fact* is seen to be expressed: $n! = fact \times count!$. We make progress towards termination by decreasing *count* by 1; observing that $n! = fact \times count \times (count - 1)!$, we see that the design role of *fact* is regained by multiplying *fact* by *count*. The resulting program, although no less efficient than the counting up version, is less satisfactory simply because its design roles are (relatively) opaque. We can also consider counting up by two, rather than by one. In this case, *fact* is restored to its design role by multiplying it by the product *count* $\times$ (*count* − 1), once *count* has been increased. Other adjustments are needed as well to take into account the parity of the input n. The resulting program is somewhat more efficient than the one we started with. Less interesting modifications, such as replacing the present *while* driver *count* <> n by *count* < n, or by *count* <= n, or reversing the order of the assignments in the *while* body (care is needed!) also suggest themselves.

Early in the course we go through many such variations of most of the programs developed. Later on, we consider alternatives that differ more profoundly. Our main intention is to make the point that students can easily consider more than a single design. We state, in terms of general engineering practice, why this is desirable, and thread a discussion of criteria for choosing among designs throughout our presentation. At another level, the aim is to impart a certain calculational skill to students and, indeed, to impart a view of programming as a calculational process—not one of trial and error. This view takes firm hold with many students exposed to this approach, and with a speed we have found to be enormously gratifying.

Begin with a Naive Solution. We have found that, late in the course, students can use the course methodology as a general tool to develop quickly preliminary solutions to hard problems. These solutions serve to lead students to the deeper understanding needed to construct better designs.

This point is best made in the context of a particular example. Engel (1993) posed the following version of an old game, attributed to Wythoff: A long playing board has marked on it two rows of columns, indexed so that the zeroth column is rightmost, and a checker is placed in each of the rows. Two players play alternately; a move consists of either moving one checker forward (that is, to the right) any number of columns in its row, or of moving both checkers forward the same number of columns in their respective rows. The loser is the one who is first faced with each checker occupying the zeroth column in its row, as no forward moves are possible from this position. We seek a program listing the losing positions, that is, the positions (i, j) from which a win is impossible, for a board with n columns. One such position is surely $(0,0)$.

Engel carries out a complete mathematical analysis, and then gives an elegant program based on that analysis. But we would instead advise our students to find a naive solution, that is, to find a program that is obviously based on the game rules. *We want the student's understanding of the problem to evolve as she designs the program, as opposed to requiring that she possess a complete mathematical understanding before even beginning to think about the program.* In our experience, the latter strategy almost always fails our students, for even moderately complex problems. In contrast, the course methodology provides students with both a starting point and a guide.

The following sketch shows how such a naive development can be begun by students acquainted with the course methodology; it also serves to display how that methodology combines naturally with top-down design to solve complex (from the standpoint of the first course) problems.

We imagine the computation as a sweep of the first row of the board, beginning at the zeroth position. At any stage, say the kth, we suppose already recorded in a list L all losing positions (p, q) with first coordinate $p \leq k$. If we can maintain this property of L invariant while increasing k from 0 to n, then all we need do when the loop terminates is to print the contents of L. If we initialize k to 0, then L can be initialized to contain just the pair $(0,0)$; any position $(0, k)$ for $k > 0$ admits a legal move to $(0,0)$ and is thus not a losing position.

Thus we see that we require a procedure *updateL,* whose task it is to add to L all losing positions with first coordinate $k + 1$. How can these positions be found? A straightforward approach is . . .

And so we are en route to outlining a program. Were we to continue, we would have a first draft, obtained top-down with the aid of the course methodology, which itself can be fleshed out using the same powerful combination of techniques. The program we have begun to sketch is far longer than Engel's. Nonetheless, it is reasonable to expect that (given suitable motivation) students will press on, using both the insight gained during their program's development, and the tables of losing positions that this first program is capable of producing, to refine the resulting program to one perhaps as brief and elegant as Engel's.

The Success of the Approach

The success of CSc 102 among CCNY students is evidenced in many ways, although we have not conducted a formal evaluation. A salient feature of the new course is its relative difficulty when compared with its predecessor: the level of the course is significantly higher, and problem sets are both more numerous and more challenging. Yet even as the course was being developed, the rate of attrition (measured as drops plus failures) fell from 34 percent to 30 percent, without the benefit of the tutoring and mentoring later made possible by an NSF grant. With subsequent fine-tuning, tutoring, and mentoring, the attrition rate has fallen to 20 percent, *even though the level of the class has increased every semester.* We point out that CSc 102 is a required course in both computer science and electrical engineering at CCNY, so the incoming student population has remained essentially unchanged during the period reflected by these numbers.

Anecdotal evidence from the five faculty in our department who have taught the new version of CSc 102 also points to success. They report that the course is much more enjoyable to teach (a typical comment is that of one colleague, Professor Lucci: "The course has restored my enthusiasm for teaching introductory programming") and that they are delighted with students' success in mastering the demanding design component of the course. We have also seen a greater preparedness of students enrolling in subsequent courses (discrete mathematics and data structures, respectively).

Another significant indicator of the success of the approach is the enthusiasm of the six community college faculty and twenty-two community college students who participated in the pilot version of a program designed to export the new course to the community colleges of the City University of New York during the summer of 1993 (Bloom, Lucci, and Troeger, 1993). An introduction to the design methodology was offered to students who had completed a year of Pascal at their home campuses in an intensive monthlong course conducted at CCNY; the class was again structured on the Treisman model, with the community college faculty serving as group leaders. In this way, two aims were realized: first, the students learned a new and better way of programming; and second, the faculty were introduced to a new way of teaching programming. All of the participating faculty are now actively exploring ways of incorporating the course methodology into their own courses.

Most important, however, is the enthusiasm of students for the new approach, as illustrated by the response of two students, described by Troeger and McCracken (in press): "These students have grade-point averages of about 2.7/4.0, and cannot by any stretch of the imagination be called top students. Yet both were deeply engaged by the course, spending lots of time on it and taking good advantage of the tutoring that was available. Then they wrote final exam papers that were simply superb. Both earned meaningful As in the course. We suspect that they were surprised at how satisfying the course was, and perhaps surprised at their success in it. We like to think that they found skills and abilities in themselves that they did not know they had."

We won't claim that every student who takes CSc 102 has such a glowing experience. But it does not take very many such cases—cases of students who could not have been described as top scholars when they entered the course—to give us the conviction that we are on to something. CSc 102 can draw out the best in students, in a way that we seldom saw in our more conventional courses.

References

Bloom, G., Lucci, S., and Troeger, D. *Project ACCESS.* Internal Report, Department of Computer Sciences, City College of New York, 1993.

Dijkstra, E. W. *A Discipline of Programming.* Englewood Cliffs, N.J.: Prentice Hall, 1976.

Engel, A. *Exploring Mathematics with Your Computer.* Vol. 35 (pp. 168–169). New Mathematical Library. Washington, D.C.: The Mathematical Association of America, 1993.

Floyd, R. W. "Assigning Meanings to Programs." In J. T. Schwartz (ed.), *Proceedings of a Symposium in Applied Mathematics.* Vol. 19: *Mathematical Aspects of Computer Science* (pp. 19–32). New York: American Mathematical Society, 1967.

Hoare, C.A.R. "An Axiomatic Basis for Computer Programming." *Communications of the ACM,* 1969, *10,* 576–580.

Treisman, U. "A Study of the Mathematics Performance of Black Students at the University of California, Berkeley." Unpublished doctoral dissertation, University of California, Berkeley, 1985.

Troeger, D. R., and McCracken, D. D. *Text for CS1* (working title). Boston: PWS Publishers, in press.

DOUGLAS R. TROEGER *is associate professor in the department of computer sciences of the City College of New York and codirector of the Center for Minorities in Information Processing Systems at City College.*

*Mechanical engineering students learn to solve ill-structured
design problems using graphic communication skills in the freshman
engineering graphics course. Integration of a critical thinking
component has guided our own iterative, interactive process of
designing a more effective teaching methodology.*

Critical Thinking and Design: Evolution of a Freshman Engineering Graphics Course

Lilia A. Sanchez, Timothy K. Hight, Joanne Gainen

Since 1990, faculty in the mechanical engineering program at Santa Clara University have been examining our design curriculum in an attempt to understand the inability of many of our students to integrate their courses and to deal effectively with open-ended or ill-structured design problems. This examination led us to define a set of skills that we felt were important to mechanical engineering designers and to redefine our goals in each course within this set of skills. After a study of cognitive theory, we also identified critical thinking as the component directly related to making decisions and to acquiring the judgment necessary for solution of open-ended problems in design. This realization led us to examine what our roles as design educators should be in helping students develop critical thinking skills and whether we could explicitly address these skills by restructuring our curriculum or our teaching methodology (Hight, Hornberger, and Sanchez, 1993).

After much discussion about integrating a design component into more of our courses, we agreed that the freshman course, Introduction to Engineering Graphics (ME 10), was an appropriate place to begin. Because we expect our students to complete a capstone project in their senior year, it seemed natural to introduce a small-scale design project to freshmen, and then integrate further design work in the sophomore and junior years. As a first step in our restructuring, we redefined the goals in the freshman course to emphasize the use of engineering graphics to communicate design ideas effectively. Our attempt to incorporate our understanding of critical thinking and its place in design education can best be related by detailing the evolution of ME 10, which the first two authors alternately teach throughout the academic year.

Background of the Course

Historically, ME 10 was a fairly standard blend of descriptive geometry, orthographic and isometric drawing, drafting and tolerances. In the mid 1980s, PC-based AUTOCAD replaced pencil and paper, but the approach and content of the course remained largely unchanged. In the latter 1980s we began to see that the course was losing relevance and that it needed to be examined and updated. We added some sketching and discussions of the design process, but the context, lectures, assignments, and exams remained the same. Our next step was to introduce a small design project. In these early attempts, we failed to realize that although our expectations for these students were fairly modest, we were asking them to tackle a design problem with little formal guidance and without any attempt on our part to relate the design project explicitly to course material. We discovered, not surprisingly, that while some rose to the occasion, many were frustrated and intimidated by the project.

A much more surprising revelation to us was most students' inability to organize material and present it effectively in a visual mode. When we asked students to make a poster presentation of their project, the majority made little effort to present the viewer with an easy-to-follow, esthetically pleasing, interesting poster. Most students did not easily make the connection between graphics and communication. It was not until we understood the tie between students' level of intellectual development, their critical thinking ability, and their inability to meet our implicit criteria that we understood their failure to "get it." We also came to understand the significance of teaching methodology in facilitating students' transition to higher levels of critical thinking.

The evolution of the course provides a case study of our own design process as we refine our teaching methodology to promote critical thinking on the part of our students, and work toward a better understanding of the relationship between critical thinking, intellectual development, and design. After briefly describing this relationship, we present the evolution of the course in more detail.

The Critical Thinking Component in Design

Design is a decision process that requires "a broad comprehensive knowledge, a rich background of experience tempered with judgment, and, most of all, creative imagination" (Shigley, 1963, p. 8). Although design is most often associated with creative thinking, Shigley's definition emphasizes the elements of judgment and decision making as well. Our subsequent study of pertinent literature led us to relate these skills to critical thinking, as defined by cognitive and educational researchers.

Critical thinking involves analyzing a problem or issue using all available information, identifying possible solutions and solution criteria, and then integrating evidence, reason, and values to arrive at a solution (Kurfiss, 1988). It requires students to construct actively their own knowledge or solution rather than rely on authority figures to tell them what to do. Students must relinquish reliance on the professor's authority and algorithmic procedures to venture forth into the unexplored territory of their own ideas early in the design process. For freshmen, who are in the early stages of their intellectual development, this is a difficult step. The developmental theories of Perry (1970) and Belenky and others (1986) helped us to understand why this is so. (Like our colleagues at the Colorado School of Mines [Pavelich, Olds, and Miller, this volume], we have come to rely on developmental theory to inform our understanding of students and our course design process. Our approach differs in its theoretical emphasis on critical thinking and in our effort to include design within a course in the traditional freshman curriculum.)

In the first level of students' development, referred to as dualism (Perry) or received knowledge (Belenky and others), students depend on authority as the source of knowledge. They seek reassurance that their design is correct and may find quite disconcerting the idea that several solutions could be effective. Holding such beliefs, they are understandably reluctant to explore new, creative ideas. This reluctance to break away from the safe guidance of authority is the first block to the design process that we felt we had to overcome.

Through continued exposure to divergent ideas, students eventually reach level 2, multiplicity/subjective knowledge, where they acknowledge that conflicting ideas are a common occurrence and then propose that *all* answers, or solutions, are equally valid because no one can say who is "right." Students at this level judge the merits of opinions and ideas subjectively, using the "inner voice" of intuition, feeling or "common sense" (Belenky and others, 1986). Level 2 thinking may be illustrated by that of the student in a machine design class who, analyzing a socket wrench assembly used to remove a bolt, has a "gut feeling" that the wrench will fail in that configuration under the specified load. When asked to justify this feeling, the student might answer, "I just know it will fail." Design students at this level may also feel that their design is a good one and that others, including the professor, have no right to criticize it because quality is purely subjective.

However, good design requires a rational basis for ideas or decisions. Students must use skills of critical thinking to evaluate the relative merits of various possible solutions to their design problem. Evaluation skills come into play as students progress to level 3, relativism/procedural knowledge. At this level, students realize that opinions differ in quality; good opinions must be grounded in good reasons, often framed as an "objective" analysis or argument. Level 3 is evident when a student design group, evaluating the feasibility of several possible solutions after a brainstorming session, defines a set of criteria that enables it to eliminate poor solutions.

The criteria may help in narrowing the choice of good solutions but do not always point to a single ideal solution. The need to choose requires a new kind of risk: commitment to an idea or course of action. Commitment in relativism (Perry, 1970)—the fourth level of intellectual maturity—is characterized by students' realization of the need to commit even when they have no external assurances of "correctness." Belenky and others describe this phase as one in which the student understands that knowledge is constructed (hence the term *constructed knowledge*) by integrating learning from others with the "inner truth" of experience and personal reflection. We see the transition to level 4 in the student design group that has reached the point where it must commit to a conceptual design but remains apprehensive about the decision it has made. The design cannot be proven correct; rather, it is a solution the students have chosen to pursue based on their knowledge, creativity, experience, intuition, and judgment.

Our ultimate goal as design educators is to facilitate the growth of our students to the highest level of critical thinking possible within our four-year curriculum. We would like them all to reach a level where they can be fully functioning, independent decision makers who can use analysis and experience to justify their decisions. Although our freshmen will not have achieved the higher levels of intellectual development in this broad sense, our design projects ask them to behave *as if* they have achieved a high level of maturity. This has proven to be a significant challenge to us and to our students. Thus an intermediate goal in each course is to guide students through the transitions between levels, if only within the limited domain of a specific design project.

To accomplish this goal, we have begun to structure our teaching to support increasingly active levels of student involvement in taking the risks of generating novel ideas, clarifying and justifying their ideas for others, and presenting the results of their decision process with pride. In this way, as described in the following section of this chapter, we believe we can begin to build students' ability to think critically and, ultimately, foster the kind of intellectual maturity that will enable them to tackle new design projects with confidence.

Evolution of ME 10

Our first attempt at strengthening the design element in the graphics course came in the fall of 1990, when the professor initiated a class discussion of design based on Polya's four-step model of problem solving (Polya, 1988). The class was then asked to apply the method to "the hardest homework problem" from any math or science course that they had that week.

With very little further discussion, the class was later given a "design" project. The last two lab assignments of the quarter were replaced by a project to design and document a tricycle to be used at the on-campus day care facility. Instructions for the project included a brief paragraph of background and justification, a set of criteria that would be used for evaluation of the design (safety, simplicity, fun, durability, creativity, and ease of manufacture), a set of pertinent geometric data (wheel sizes, wheelbase, and so on), and assignment requirements (create a design, orthographic and isometric assembly drawings of the complete trike, detail drawings of two components). The completed projects were presented as paper designs to be evaluated by the professor.

Of the approximately seventy-five tricycles designed, most were slight variations, at best, of standard models. Ten to twenty of the designs could be considered imaginative, only a handful really interesting. The drawings were generally done to satisfy the minimum standards. Although the students were, in general, interested in the project and spent more time on this project than they would have on standard lab assignments, they did not really know how to approach the problem, generate new ideas, or screen the ideas that they did have. Very little critical thinking, design, or problem solving seemed to be in evidence.

There was also little evidence that most students were comfortable using their own ideas or intuition. Without specific guidance to do otherwise, the students relied heavily on what they could see existing in the world. By doing what was required by the "authority," and staying in the safe zone of familiar designs, the students evidenced critical thinking behavior consistent with the first level of intellectual development. By throwing this design problem at them, we had managed to get their attention and interest, but we probably had not furthered development of their critical thinking skills.

In the fall of 1992, a further evolution occurred. We made a conscious effort to alter the tone and direction of the course. We emphasized sketching, visualization techniques, and design at the expense of descriptive geometry. A new text (Rodriguez, 1992) provided good integration of the new topics and helped us define the philosophy that we wanted to adopt in the course.

We also introduced a simplified design process (finding a need, defining a problem, gathering information, generating ideas, deciding between alternatives, and designing in detail) and developed some sample scenarios in class. Students were assigned to create a personal "bug list," which they would use as the basis for selecting a design project due at the end of the quarter. They were encouraged to pick fairly simple problems (or "bugs") that were mechanical or geometric in nature so that the solution could be shown clearly in orthographic or isometric drawing. We conducted a brainstorming exercise in class so they could practice generating novel ideas for a design problem.

Although we had given the project more emphasis, there was still little evidence that the eighty students in the course that quarter had gained confidence in their own ideas or that they were willing to explore sketching or risky designs. The problems they chose were often frivolous—for example, a beer mug with a hidden compartment, a simple skateboard, a pen and pencil holder. Most of the design solutions were simple, even simplistic, probably the first idea that occurred to the student. The students again seemed to remain at the first, safety-oriented level of critical thinking, dualism/received knowledge.

We were puzzled at the time that the students did not make connections on their own and attack the design problem with their new array of skills. In hindsight, the lectures and exercises did not communicate to students how the skills of sketching and brainstorming related to the design process, especially to finding a need, defining the problem, and generating alternatives, or to the ultimate goal of creating and communicating solutions to problems. We would later come to understand that we had not adequately prepared students to make the transition from the received knowledge level to the more exploratory and analytical forms of levels 2 and 3.

The next iteration of the design project, implemented in the winter of 1993, added a new level of challenge: students were required to prepare a poster to present their designs to the class. The project was no longer "for the professor's eyes only." Instead of a final exam, each student would fill out a short written evaluation of all the projects during the poster session held at the end of the quarter. We thought that the added element of sharing ideas with one's peers would spark more interest in the assignment and raise the level of performance. We stressed that the project should be personal, did not have to be complicated, and was to be communicated using the graphics techniques learned in the class. This time, we emphasized relationships between topics covered in lectures (for example, sketching, orthographic drawings, dimensioning, and isometric drawings) and the processes of design and presentation of ideas.

The results were again disappointing. The majority of the forty students in that quarter's class picked safe problems on familiar territory—for example, toothpaste dispensers, compact disc racks, desks that used space more efficiently, dorm space-saving devices, and laundry or shower caddies. The students did not show much concern for the esthetics of the posters, often omitting titles, using little color, applying handwritten labels, and showing little sense of visual organization. Ownership of the design was not always clear because the students' names were often not visible. Students relied heavily on written text rather than sketches to communicate both the problem and the new design solution. Some had only orthographic drawings, the technique they were most comfortable using because it was done on the computer workstations and was the mode used most often in lab exercises. In many instances, it was not clear how the new design functioned or what was new about it. Students seemed unable to take the perspective of a viewer attempting to understand their design and presented their ideas as if the meaning would be obvious to all, so no further explanation—or in this case, visualization—was necessary.

In terms of critical thinking levels, the typical response from the students in this quarter was again at level 1: doing little sketching for fear of making a bad sketch, relying on written text, and choosing very safe problems for fear of making a mistake. Like many students at this level, they chose to play it safe until they could figure out "the Answer" (what the professor wants).

Not yet cognizant of the developmental foundations of critical thinking, we had increased the challenge of the project by requiring a poster but had not significantly increased support for the learning process. We underestimated how much formal guidance would be necessary to help students meet the challenge. We were again attempting to introduce design on a small scale to these students using a sink-or-swim approach.

The design project assignment the following quarter, spring 1993, remained the same for the forty students that quarter, but by this time our concurrent study of the developmental foundations of critical thinking had helped us to reexamine and redesign our teaching methodology. We began to see that students needed more explicit guidance to make what we assumed were obvious connections between lecture topics, lab and class exercises and the design project. Classroom activities and lectures were modified accordingly to strengthen students' understanding of graphical communication of design ideas. We took greater care to explain each graphic technique in the context of communicating a design idea. The design process, brainstorming, and sketching were discussed more explicitly within the context of the design project. In an attempt to introduce multiplicity and reduce egocentrism, we displayed posters from the previous quarter. The posters allowed us to illustrate the range of possible projects, the multiplicity of opinions and design ideas, the use of different engineering graphic modes, the variety of presentation styles, and the effective or ineffective communication of designs. By using examples of their peers' work, and inviting class discussion and opinions, we encouraged the expansion of students' own perspectives and implicitly invited *them* to be the judges. An acceptance of different perspectives is the basis of level 2 intellectual development as defined in our adaptation of the Perry and the Belenky and others' models; it is essential for critical thinking because students begin to free themselves from the tyranny of reliance on authority, need for safety, and passive acceptance of the "right answer."

That quarter's approach did, in fact, stimulate greater richness in the projects. The problems were more varied and involved more personally meaningful bugs, including a classroom desk–chair for both right-handed and left-handed people, a compact night stand/shelf for a dormitory bunk bed, an in-ear headphone set. Students were more likely to sketch in an attempt, although minimal, to make their concepts clear. The esthetics of the posters improved; students used more color and better organization, relied less on text to explain ideas, and became more creative in their selection of presentation styles.

We interpreted these improvements to mean that students were more willing to depart from safe and familiar territory, suggesting that classroom activities such as viewing and critically discussing other students' work helped our students to make the transition from a level 1 (dualism/received knowledge) to a level 2 (multiplicity/subjective knowledge) approach to the design problem.

Building on these changes in the following term, fall 1993, we included a more detailed discussion of the different types of engineering graphics and their relevance to the design project, that is, sketching to illustrate the design problem, isometric drawing to illustrate the design solution, and orthographic drawings to detail the design solution. Classroom activities included brainstorming or sketching exercises in which judgment was suspended by both the professor and the students. Each student was required to keep a sketchbook and a standing class assignment was to draw two sketches per week. Fluency in expressing ideas was emphasized in sketching assignments. Lectures included explicit descriptions of design problems as open-ended problems having many solutions. Students were encouraged to examine their everyday activities and surroundings to select a personally meaningful design problem.

To help the students understand the design process and the effective communication of ideas, the professor presented and evaluated posters from previous quarters. She pointed out the originality of the design, the organization and esthetics of the poster, the engineering graphics styles used, the presentation of the bug and design solution in context rather than as isolated drawings, the clarity of the function of the design solution, and the dependence on sketches rather than written text to communicate the problem or solution. The discussion was intended to give students more explicit criteria derived from concrete examples.

The result was that the majority of the eighty posters presented in that quarter more effectively communicated the students' designs and incorporated various types of engineering graphics than had earlier designs. Students seemed less concerned with "the right answer" or "a good sketch." More sketching was apparent as students realized its importance to a viewer's understanding of the design projects. The projects seemed to broaden in range and challenge and truly seemed to be "personal bugs" for the students—for example, a bike rack for pickup trucks, "safe" dividers (used for drafting) with retractable points, an "odorless" fish food grinder/feeder. The esthetics and originality of the posters were enhanced. The students seemed truly to enjoy and to become invested in the project and the experience of the design process. In fact, several carried the assignment further and developed prototypes as they anticipated the next step in the design process.

We felt this group generally demonstrated a level 2 response to the project (multiplicity/subjective knowledge), with many individuals using skills characteristic of level 3 (relativism/procedural knowledge). The posters reflected students' willingness to trust their inner voices in selecting the projects as they exhibited more risk taking and less wariness of authority's judgment. The increased effectiveness in communicating the design problem and solutions suggests that the students have begun to use criteria to evaluate and refine their work, typical of level 3 critical thinking (procedural knowledge).

The next iteration of the design project, implemented in winter 1994, took a new approach to helping students develop criteria for effective communication of design ideas. Groups of four to five students were given a poster from a previous quarter to examine and critique. They were asked to explain the project to the class, as they understood it from the poster; to comment on the presentation style, the effectiveness of communication, the design idea; and to make suggestions for improvement. This exercise encouraged the students to establish criteria and procedures for evaluating the posters, a step intended to spur transition to level 3 critical thinking (relativism/procedural knowledge). The class-generated checklist included esthetics, logical flow of ideas, appropriate graphic styles for presentation of bug, design solution, and assembly or functioning of design solution.

Instruction in the winter term also included more sketching to build confidence in that skill, more classroom exercises to guide students through the ideation phase of the design process, and setting milestones for the project.

The criteria exercise seemed most useful to students in planning the poster and in making the connection between appropriate graphic styles and the communication of design ideas. By placing them in the role of observer and critic, we enabled them not only to evaluate one another's posters but also to better comprehend the basis for judging and improving their own. They seemed less concerned with what the professor expected, more focused on what was necessary for an effective presentation to any observer. This was a significant transition to level 3 critical thinking for many students.

As in the previous quarter, the forty posters more effectively communicated design ideas. The overall presentations were markedly improved, as students paid more attention to esthetics and logical flow of ideas, to sketching the bug and solution in context, and to using more appropriately different graphics styles. The selection of projects again seemed to be more challenging and diverse, including such projects as an "EZ" flip water bottle replacer, an adjustable armrest, and a no-hands doorknob. Several students built prototypes of their design solutions.

We judged the students' responses in this quarter, in terms of critical thinking, to be generally at level 3. The students exhibited more risk taking as they selected projects that were more personal. The greater use of all the graphic styles, especially sketching, seems to indicate that they have begun to use procedural knowledge in the selection of the appropriate graphic style. More attention to the esthetics and the overall presentation seems to indicate that they had recognized their importance in the effective communication of a design to others.

Future Work

The next iteration of the course will include use of an instrument to assess the students' development according to Perry's levels combined with more documentation by the students of their design process, such as a journal to include a bug list; brainstorming sessions; more sketching in the ideation phase; preliminary drawings; and so on. A review of this information in concert with the final projects will give us a better understanding of whether the course promotes transition to higher levels of development as applied to the project domain. In addition, we plan to begin discussions of how subsequent courses in the curriculum support and reinforce the development that now has begun to occur in our freshman-level course.

References

Belenky, M. F., Clinchy, B. M., Goldberger, N., and Tarule, J. M. *Women's Ways of Knowing: The Development of Self, Voice, and Mind.* New York: Basic Books, 1986.

Hight, T. K., Hornberger, L., and Sanchez, L. A. "Toward Critical Thinking Mechanical Designers." *Proceedings of the Fifth International Conference on Design Theory and Methodology, DTM '93.* Albuquerque, N.M.: Design, Theory, and Methodology, 1993.

Kurfiss, J. G. *Critical Thinking: Theory, Research, Practice, and Possibilities.* ASHE-ERIC higher education report no. 2. Washington, D.C.: Association for the Study of Higher Education, 1988.

Perry, W. G., Jr. *Forms of Intellectual and Ethical Development in the College Years: a Scheme.* New York: Holt, Rinehart & Winston, 1970.

Polya, G. *How to Solve It: A New Aspect of Mathematical Method.* (2nd ed.) Princeton, N.J.: Princeton University Press, 1988.

Rodriguez, W. *The Modeling of Design Ideas: Graphics and Visualization Techniques for Engineers.* New York: McGraw-Hill, 1992.

Shigley, J. E. *Mechanical Design.* New York: McGraw-Hill, 1963.

LILIA A. SANCHEZ is assistant professor of mechanical engineering at Santa Clara University. She teaches engineering design courses at the undergraduate and graduate level. Her research interests include holography, kinematics, and human joint motion.

TIMOTHY K. HIGHT is associate professor of mechanical engineering at Santa Clara University. He teaches undergraduate and graduate level design courses, and conducts research in recycling packaging material, design methodology, finite element analysis, and computer graphic solid modeling.

JOANNE GAINEN is director of the Teaching and Learning Center at Santa Clara University.

*This chapter considers some women's surprising responses to an
introductory physics sequence in which lectures are abandoned in
favor of activity-based collaborative work enhanced by the use of
integrated computer tools.*

Women's Responses to an Activity-Based Introductory Physics Program

*Priscilla W. Laws, Pamela J. Rosborough,
Frances J. Poodry*

These are exciting times for physics educators. Ten years ago most physics
instructors were largely unaware of the outcomes of research in physics education. Today, several curricula have been developed on the basis of educational research, including physics by inquiry and tutorials in introductory
physics developed at the University of Washington (McDermott, 1993), tools
for scientific thinking developed at Tufts University (Thornton, 1986), real-
time physics developed at the University of Oregon (Sokoloff, 1991), and
workshop physics developed at Dickinson College (Laws, 1986, 1990, 1991a,
1991b). These nontraditional, activity-based curricula are considered "constructivist" because they cultivate scientific reasoning ability and the development of conceptual models by engaging students in the process of making
predictions and observations and then constructing qualitative models that can
help them understand patterns in the observations. These reasoning processes
are enhanced by discussions with peers, teaching assistants, and instructors.

One important issue in evaluating the efficacy of new activity-based introductory physics curricula is whether they have the potential to help us close
the gap between the number of men and women who choose to major in
physics or study more science. In a study entitled *Women's Ways of Knowing*
(Belenky, Clinchy, Goldberger, and Tarule, 1986), the authors state, "Most of

Curriculum development and dissemination have been supported by the Fund for the
Improvement of Postsecondary Education and the National Science Foundation. Some of
the workshop physics materials and computer tools were developed collaboratively with
Ronald Thornton and David Sokoloff.

the women we interviewed were drawn to the sort of knowledge that emerges from firsthand observation" (p. 200) and that educators should "stress collaboration over debate" (p. 229). The present chapter asks: How might constructivist, activity-based physics courses in which collaborative learning is emphasized affect the attitudes and achievement of women who take them? Since 41 percent of the students who have enrolled in the calculus-based workshop physics courses at Dickinson are women, we have had an unusual opportunity to study the impact of activity-based courses on them.

In the first part of this chapter we describe the design of the calculus-based workshop physics curriculum. Then we discuss the impact of these courses on student learning and attitudes. Finally, we address questions pertaining to the experiences of the Dickinson College women enrolled in these courses.

The Workshop Physics Curriculum

The workshop physics project at Dickinson College was developed to address the major problems in the teaching and learning of introductory physics courses—failure to deal effectively with students' profound misconceptions about physical phenomena, the cognitive overload that comes when too much material is covered, and the absence of contemporary tools for the construction and communication of scientific knowledge (Laws, 1990, 1991a, 1991b).

We believe that the acquisition of transferable skills of scientific inquiry is more important than either problem solving or the comprehensive transmission of descriptive knowledge about introductory physics topics. Workshop physics courses are therefore cooperative and activity-centered. Observations, direct experience, and computers help students to build the physical intuition needed to understand vital concepts. The shift to an emphasis on inquiry skills is based on the observation that most introductory physics students do not have enough experience with everyday phenomena to relate concrete experience to scientific explanation. A second reason for emphasizing inquiry skills is that when one is confronted with the task of learning an expanding field of knowledge, the only viable strategy is to acquire independent investigation skills to be implemented as needed.

Although lectures and demonstrations are useful alternatives to reading for transmitting information and teaching specific skills, they do not help students learn how to think critically, conduct scientific inquiry, or acquire real experience with natural phenomena. Peers are often more helpful to students than instructors are in facilitating original thinking and problem solving. The time that is often spent passively listening to lectures would be better spent in direct inquiry with peers. The role of the instructor in this model is to shape a creative learning environment, lead discussions, and engage in dialogue with students. Computer spreadsheets along with sensors and special software facilitate student-directed collection, analysis, and graphical display of data. Students also use computers for problem solving and mathematical modeling.

All of the introductory physics courses have been taught in a workshop format at Dickinson College since the 1987–88 academic year.

Curricular Materials and Course Organization

In workshop physics courses at Dickinson College, students meet in three two-hour sessions each week. Each section has one instructor, two undergraduate teaching assistants, and up to twenty-four students. Each pair of students shares the use of a microcomputer and an extensive collection of scientific apparatus and other gadgets. Although students work in pairs at the computer, they collaborate in groups of four for laboratory observations and experiments. Among other things, students pitch baseballs, whack bowling balls with rubber hammers, break pine boards with their bare hands, build electronic circuits, and ignite paper by compressing air. The workshop labs are staffed during evening and weekend hours with undergraduate assistants.

Traditional content in the calculus-based courses has been reduced by about 25 percent. The material has been broken up into units lasting about one week, and students use an activity guide (Laws, 1986) that has expositions, questions, and instructions as well as blank spaces for student data, calculations, and reflections. The activity guide has been used both with a number of traditional introductory physics textbooks and without a text at Dickinson College and elsewhere. In our two semester calculus-based course sequence at Dickinson, we complete twenty-seven units spanning topics in mechanics, heat and temperature, and electricity and magnetism.

We often use a four-part learning sequence described by cognitive psychologist David Kolb (1984). Students usually begin a topic with an examination of their own preconceptions and then make qualitative observations. After some reflection and discussion, the instructor helps with the development of definitions and mathematical theories. The study of a topic usually ends with quantitative experimentation centered around verification of mathematical theories.

Student Learning and Attitudes

Dickinson College is a private, residential four-year liberal arts college with a total enrollment of about nineteen hundred students. The two main subpopulations enrolled in the physics sequence have different reasons for taking physics and, as we have learned, different experiences of and responses to the workshop approach. Over half these students are freshmen and sophomores who are often considering a major in mathematics, computer science, or science. The typical junior or senior student is taking physics to prepare for medical school or graduate work in chemistry or biology.

Numerous instruments have been used to assess the workshop physics program, including the following: (1) conceptual learning examinations developed at other universities; (2) standard Dickinson course evaluation forms;

(3) evaluation of the results of a multi-institution introductory physics attitudes questionnaire administered by us in the fall of 1989 and 1990; (4) tracking of student performance on homework and problem sections of examinations; (5) interviews with a cross section of women who were taking or had completed calculus-based workshop physics courses; and (6) interviews with transfer students and some of our graduates who had completed the calculus-based workshop physics sequence.

After workshop physics was introduced, more students mastered concepts that are considered difficult to teach because they involve classic misconceptions. Students taking traditional courses usually cannot answer certain questions that physics teachers view as obvious. For example, at time of enrollment in introductory physics, 90 percent to 100 percent of students at Dickinson believe that just after its release there is a special upward force on a tossed coin. Physicists believe that the only force on the coin as it moves up and then down is downward force due to the gravitational attraction of the earth. *Posttests have shown that traditional instruction at Dickinson and elsewhere changes the notions of only about 10 percent of the students.* In contrast, about 80 percent to 90 percent of the students can answer new questions based on the coin toss concept after taking workshop physics. Our studies at Dickinson have confirmed the findings of a number of physics education researchers. In general, a small percentage of students (0 percent to 30 percent) answer questions that are counterintuitive correctly before the study of physics. Posttests reveal that traditional instruction affects only 5 percent to 10 percent of the students who answer these questions incorrectly on pretests. After workshop physics courses at Dickinson, 50 percent to 90 percent of the students answer these counterintuitive questions correctly on posttests.

We also know by observation and survey responses that students who complete workshop physics are very comfortable working in a laboratory setting and working with computers. This competency with the tools of exploration and analysis is often noted by visitors from other institutions who visit our classrooms during the second semester of our two-semester sequence.

To evaluate the impact of the workshop physics teaching methods on students, a survey of student attitudes toward various learning experiences was developed in the fall of 1989. This survey was administered in December 1989 to almost four hundred students at eight colleges and universities, and again in December 1990 to more than twenty-eight hundred students at fourteen institutions including Dickinson. The survey asks students to rate the value of learning experiences such as reading textbooks, attending lectures, using computers, and so on; to rate self-reported gains in skill level and knowledge; and to compare their attitudes toward the physical sciences and computers before and after having taken the first semester of college introductory physics.

The attitude survey indicates that Dickinson College workshop physics students are more positive about their mastery of computer applications as a result of the courses than about any other aspect of them, and that they view computer skills as useful in many contexts outside of physics. In addition, workshop physics students rate a whole range of learning experiences more highly than do their cohorts taking traditional courses. For example, when students are asked to rate the value of fifteen learning opportunities, such as attending lectures, using computers, watching demonstrations, solving textbook problems or doing experiments, workshop physics students rate all of these activities—except solving textbook problems, reading the textbook, and attending lectures—more highly than students taking introductory physics courses at other liberal arts colleges. They are significantly more positive about the value of observations and laboratory experiments than students taking traditional courses. This may reflect the fact that observations and experiments account for a larger proportion of their grade.

Although most freshmen prefer the workshop approach, we have been disheartened by the fact that about 20 percent of our students thoroughly dislike it and state emphatically that they would prefer a return to the lecture approach. Roughly half of the upperclass chemistry and biology majors fall in this group. Many of the students who say they would prefer lectures resent having to "teach themselves everything." Although the percentage of students who dislike workshop physics is lower than the percentage of students who used to be hostile about our traditional lecture-based courses, we are attempting to achieve a better understanding of why some still become hostile as a result of their experiences. We are beginning with our present focus on the experiences of women.

How Women Respond to Workshop Physics

One important outcome of the workshop physics program is that eligible women are choosing to major in physics at a slightly higher rate than eligible men. However, their responses to the program differ in some respects from those of the male students. Data on sex differences are based on survey responses from the 1990 cohort at Dickinson College, which included twenty-four men and twenty-two women. Although the sample size is small, the results are consistent with observations in other years.

In the survey, students used a five-point scale to express how they remembered feeling about using computers before taking physics and then to rate how they felt after taking a semester of physics. One of the most dramatic differences between men and women in the 1990 survey was initial reluctance of the freshman and sophomore women to use computers. However, at the end of one semester the feelings of these freshman and sophomore women went from a rather negative 2.5 to a quite positive 4.0. In contrast, the average of both the junior and senior women and all of the men started out quite positive, that is, 3.7 or 3.8 in each case, and became slightly more positive, that is, 3.9 or 4.0 in each case.

Gender differences also surfaced in the Dickinson women's attitudes toward laboratory activities. Even though average grades for men and women are about the same, women valued their learning opportunities more than men. However, the women who took calculus-based workshop physics at Dickinson in 1990 were less confident than the men about their laboratory skills, which included using sensors attached to the computer, using spread-sheet and graphing tools, making observations and doing experiments, having class discussions, and writing lab reports. All five lab experiences were valued more highly at Dickinson than they were at any of the other institutions in the survey, and there were no noticeable gender differences in these ratings at other institutions. However, the twenty-four women taking workshop physics at Dickinson in the fall of 1990 rated these experiences more highly than men (3.9 versus 3.4). These women also rated themselves at 3.0 on learning gains in lab-related skills whereas their male counterparts rated their gains at 4.2.

We were dismayed to find that some women taking workshop physics in December 1990 became significantly more negative about laboratory work after the first semester. Closer examination of the data showed that the junior and senior women became *very* negative about the laboratory experience during the semester while the freshman and sophomore women became slightly more positive. The freshman and sophomore women started out less positive than the men, yet ended up with the same feelings about lab work as their male counterparts. The responses of various groups are shown in Table 8.1.

Women's Voices: Why Is Lab Work Unpleasant?

We were discouraged but not totally surprised by the fact that, according to the 1990 survey, the junior and senior women became more negative about hands-on laboratory work as a result of taking the first semester of the workshop physics course sequence. Course evaluations and instructor observations have made us aware that juniors and seniors preparing for medical school or graduate school in biology and chemistry tend to be more negative about the program than the freshmen and sophomores. We realized that many of these women, especially the premeds, are under pressure to get top grades and do not see a connection between what they are learning in physics and their professions. We guessed that the extensive use of computers as part of the lab work might prove to be one of the "turn-offs" for some of these women.

We decided to interview groups of women to learn more about their perspectives on the course. Three groups, each including five women, were chosen randomly from a list of students still enrolled at Dickinson College who

Table 8.1. Students' Feelings About Laboratory Work Before and After One Semester of Calculus-Based Workshop Physics (Fall 1990, Dickinson College)

Group	N	Before	After	Change
Freshman/Sophomore Women	12	3.2	3.6	0.4
Freshman/Sophomore Men	18	3.6	3.5	−0.1
Junior/Senior Women	9	3.0	2.0	−1.0
Junior/Senior Men	5	2.4	3.4	1.0

had taken or were currently enrolled in one of the calculus-based workshop physics courses. Participants were informed that their participation in the study would be strictly anonymous and each participant received a modest stipend for her time. Each group met for about an hour in April 1992 for an unstructured discussion moderated by Pam Rosborough.

Responses from all three groups mirrored those of Dickinson women compiled from the attitude survey. Specifically, after having taken the course, attitudes toward the computer became more positive for thirteen out of fifteen women in our study and remained the same for two women. In the case of feelings toward working in the physics laboratory, six out of fifteen women revealed a pronounced decrease in positive attitude after having taken the course, six out of fifteen indicated a positive change in attitude, and three women remained unchanged in their attitudes. Even though many of the women interviewed felt positive about working in the laboratory in retrospect, a sufficient number expressed negative feelings to enable us to get a clearer sense of the sources of these negative perceptions.

Many of the frustrations involved stressful collaborations. The women worked in groups of two to four students whom they either chose to work with or ended up with. Some of these groups included men, others were single-sex. Commenting on their groups, these women complained of domineering partners, clashes in temperament, subjection to ridicule, fears that their partners didn't respect them, and feelings that their partners understood far more than they did. They often felt guilty about putting their needs ahead of those of their partners. Some women were frustrated by the domineering behavior of lab partners (both male and female). The following is one example:

> Last semester my lab partner always ended up entering the spreadsheet formulas and I wanted a chance but I was never quite bold enough to take control. . . . I always found it a problem to divide the labor . . . . You never know who's doing more—you never know if the other person's angry.

They often felt guilty about burdening partners with their needs, especially when they felt their own mastery was inferior:

> I had a lab partner . . . and she was really smart. She knew so much more than me. I'd think she'd get frustrated with me . . . . Sometimes she would sit there and explain to me over and over and I just wouldn't pick up on it.

At other times, the clashes were specific to the lab situation. For example,

> My lab partner and I are the best of friends but . . . when we had physics, and again sometimes when we'd do our homework, we hated each other.

Collaboration, at times, brought out basic cultural problems concerning respect:

My lab partner and I had two very overbearing male lab partners in our group.
. . . They even went so far as to suggest that she go to the snack bar to get us
food when they thought she came up with a really silly answer.

Another source of frustration expressed primarily by premeds is the belief that
getting As is critical and that "learning is about right answers," a view characterized as "received knowing" by Belenky, Clinchy, Goldberger and Tarule
(1986). Most of the junior and senior women enrolled in the workshop physics
courses had received good grades in both high school and college-level science
courses by working diligently to memorize accepted facts and procedures. In
contrast, the freshman and sophomore women who come to the course early
in their college careers are considering a major in a physical science or mathematics. They have been told that college is going to be challenging, and they
seem more open to the process of constructing meaning from their own
experiences. One interviewee expressed her views this way:

I found in my class that the upperclassmen were more frustrated than the freshmen were because you came in and you had other science classes where you'd
been taught in a traditional way and they expect you to learn in a totally different way and it's frustrating. I'm a premed and I've talked to a lot of other people who are premed and we all felt the same way. We've been conditioned to
learn in a certain kind of way and we weren't learning that way. When you come
in as a freshman, I think it's easier.

Premeds especially disliked the fact that lab exercises required them to make
predictions that sometimes turned out to be wrong. Even though they were
not graded down for incorrect predictions, they resisted this approach because
they were accustomed to the reinforcement of getting right answers at every
step of the way. This problem is not unique to women. A number of male
premeds have voiced the same complaints. However, the results of the 1990
attitude survey and our impressions in other years lead us to believe that
women, more than men, have been encouraged to view learning as straightforward fact gathering or memorization.

Although the multi-institution survey revealed that the time demands of
the workshop physics courses were no greater than those of courses at other
institutions, a number of the women we interviewed complained about exces-
sive and uncertain time demands. Concerns about time demands were inter-
twined with the view of learning as knowing the "right" answers, as in one
woman's complaint about having to "put so much time into something that
isn't straightforward when I could be doing so many other things that would
be straightforward." Some concerns about time were unique to women: they
found it stressful to have to return to the lab at night when an experiment
wasn't working. As one interviewee observed,

It's not just the workload and that expectations are high . . . because that's a given for both men and women. The men have more free time because they tend to be involved with fewer activities.

In spite of these concerns, none of the women complained about the learning atmosphere being competitive, and they felt that after the first few weeks they were as capable as the men when it came to using the scientific apparatus and computers.

Conclusions

The calculus-based workshop physics courses at Dickinson College are more successful than traditional introductory physics courses when overall improvements in student attitudes and conceptual learning are considered. A woman who takes these courses during the freshman and sophomore year has the same likelihood of choosing to major in physics as her male counterpart. Women who complete the workshop physics calculus-based introductory course sequence feel they are as good as men at working with apparatus and computers. However, junior and senior women as a group tend to find the laboratory work in workshop physics courses more stressful and unpleasant than other students do.

From interviews with women who have taken one or more semesters of workshop physics, we found that those who are unhappy with workshop physics have difficulties with collaborative work, feel stressed about the time demands of physics, and understand learning as received rather than constructed knowledge (Belenky, Clinchy, Goldberger, and Tarule, 1986). Many of these unhappy students feel that the instructor should make learning straightforward and uncomplicated, without requiring peer collaboration or intellectual struggle. An additional factor involves the perception that getting As in physics is critical to future success. Any attempt to change the rules for succeeding is very stressful to students who are not confident intellectually.

We were surprised by our students' responses to collaborative work. Some of the women we interviewed found it stressful to work with assertive people, and some noted that putting their own needs ahead of others made them feel guilty. On the one hand our findings are surprising because women are assumed to like collaborative work more than men do and to be better at it. On the other hand our findings are not surprising in the face of a growing literature about women being more sensitive than men to the needs and opinions of others (Gilligan, 1982; Light, 1990), about women lacking intellectual confidence in the sciences after years of socialization (Kahle and Lakes, 1983; Sadker and Sadker, 1994), about the greater sensitivity of women to grade stresses and competition (Manis, Stoat, Thomas, and Davis, 1989; Seymour, 1992; Tobias, 1990), and about the problems encountered in college courses by both men and women in earlier stages of intellectual development (Belenky, Clinchy, Goldberger, and Tarule, 1986; Perry, 1970).

What has our workshop physics experience taught us about the potential for activity-based constructivist science courses to attract more women to the study of science? Although we had a small statistical sample in our survey, the cumulative course evaluations and interviews lead us to believe that women who take workshop physics courses early in their college careers like them better than traditional physics courses. They are just as academically successful and positive about the courses as—if not more positive than—their male counterparts. Unfortunately, these findings do not seem to be true for women who take these courses as upperclassmen.

What can we do in activity-based courses to attract more women to the study of physics and related sciences? We feel that students should take as many courses as possible that encourage reasoning and direct observations *early* in their schooling. Students, especially girls and women, should find constructivist approaches to learning helpful in reaching career goals. It would help if achievement examinations, like MCAT and GRE, emphasized scientific reasoning ability over straightforward content-based and procedural knowledge. We must take steps to promote educational reform at all levels and in all subject areas so that students understand how vital and empowering the process of constructing scientific knowledge can be.

Instructors should be conscious of shaping experiences for both male and female students that are cooperative and noncompetitive, offer engaging and challenging activities, have reasonable workloads, and enable students to work in a safe and comfortable environment. However, despite our efforts to provide these experiences for students in our workshop physics courses, some of our women students are still unhappy with our approach. Devising effective methods for rendering activity-based courses less stressful is not easy. Sensitivity on the part of instructors to group dynamics and the organization of groups may improve students' experiences in collaborative work.

We feel that a lack of personal and academic confidence is an important factor in making collaborative work difficult for some students. If activity-based courses involving collaborative knowledge construction were started early in the elementary years and continued through the college level, especially in other college science courses, more women, especially junior and senior women, would be receptive to and successful using the modes of learning emphasized in courses such as workshop physics. In the long run, students who have had positive experiences with collaborative work in other constructivist courses should better appreciate the benefits of collaboration in workshop physics courses.

References

Belenky, M. F., Clinchy, B. M., Goldberger, N., and Tarule, J. M. *Women's Ways of Knowing: The Development of Self, Voice, and Mind.* New York: Basic Books, 1986.

Gilligan, C. *In a Different Voice.* Cambridge, Mass.: Harvard University Press, 1982.

Kahle, J. B., and Lakes, M. K. "The Myth of Equality in Science Classrooms." *Journal of Research in Science Teaching,* 1983, *20* (2), 131–140.

Kolb, D. *Experiential Learning: Experience as the Source of Learning and Development.* Englewood Cliffs, N.J.: Prentice Hall, 1984.

Laws, P. W. *Workshop Physics Activity Guide.* Portland, Ore.: Vernier Software, 1986.

Laws, P. W. "Workshop Physics—Replacing Lectures with Real Experience." *Proceedings of the Conference on Computers in Physics Instruction.* Reading, Mass.: Addison-Wesley, 1990.

Laws, P. W. "Workshop Physics: Learning Introductory Physics by Doing It." *Change,* July/Aug. 1991a.

Laws, P. W. "Calculus-Based Physics Without Lectures." *Physics Today,* Dec. 1991b.

Light, R. J. *The Harvard Assessment Seminars: Explorations with Students and Faculty about Teaching, Learning, and Student Life.* First Report. Cambridge, Mass.: Harvard University Press, 1990.

Manis, J. M., Stoat, B. F., Thomas, N. G., and Davis, C. S. *An Analysis of Factors Affecting Choices Affecting Majors in Science, Mathematics, and Engineering at the University of Michigan.* CEW research report no. 23. Ann Arbor: University of Michigan Center for Continuing Education of Women, July 1989.

McDermott, L. C. "Guest Comment: How We Teach and How Students Learn—A Mismatch?" *American Journal of Physics,* 1993, *61* (4), 295–298.

Perry, W. G., Jr. *Forms of Intellectual and Ethical Development in the College Years: A Scheme.* Troy, Mo.: Holt, Rinehart & Winston, 1970.

Sadker, M., and Sadker, D. *Failing at Fairness: How America's Schools Cheat Girls.* New York: Scribner's, 1994.

Seymour, E. "Undergraduate Problems with Teaching and Advising in SME Majors—Explaining Gender Differences in Attrition Rates." *Journal of College Science Teaching,* Mar./Apr. 1992, pp. 284–292.

Sokoloff, D. R. *RealTime Physics.* Portland, Ore.: Vernier Software, 1991.

Thornton, R. K. *Tools for Scientific Thinking.* Portland, Ore.: Vernier Software, 1986.

Thornton, R. K., and Sokoloff, D. R. "Learning Motion Concepts Using Real-Time Microcomputer-Based Laboratory Tools." *American Journal of Physics,* 1990, *58* (9), 858–866.

Tobias, S. *They're Not Dumb, They're Different: Stalking the Second Tier.* Tucson, Ariz.: Research Corporation, 1990.

PRISCILLA W. LAWS *is professor of physics and director of the nationally recognized workshop physics curriculum development project at Dickinson College (Carlisle, Pennsylvania). She holds a Ph.D. in theoretical nuclear physics.*

PAMELA J. ROSBOROUGH *is a counselor at the Stevens Mental Health Center (Carlisle, Pennsylvania). She served as manager of the workshop physics project from 1990 to 1993.*

FRANCES J. POODRY *was a workshop physics project evaluator in the summers of 1991 and 1992. She teaches physics and physical science courses at the Abraham Lincoln High School (Philadelphia).*

A new approach to introductory accounting teaches students to view issues from a variety of perspectives, broadens their exposure to unstructured problems with more than one possible solution approach, and places accounting measurement in a real-world context.

Introductory Accounting: Changing the First Course

Karen V. Pincus

From the mid 1960s to the late 1980s business schools across the nation experienced an unprecedented period of growth. From 1966 to 1987, the number of incoming freshmen expressing interest in a business major more than doubled, growing from 11.6 percent to 25.6 percent, according to the annual American Freshman Survey sponsored by the American Council on Education. But as the 1990s began, the trend started to reverse rapidly. By 1991, only 15.6 percent of entering freshmen planned to study business. In 1993, the American Association of Collegiate Schools of Business reported that among its member schools only 16 percent of entering freshmen planned to major in business, compared with 25 percent just five years earlier. This declining interest in business majors also exacerbates a long-standing problem of too few minority students attracted to careers in business.

Although outside influences—including changing political and economic conditions—may account for some of the decreased interest in business majors, there is growing concern that the decline comes in part from a failure of educational programs to keep pace with changes in the business world and society in general. Students, it is argued, are being given a false and incomplete picture of the role they will play if they pursue business careers. This distorted picture unjustly discourages some students from choosing a business major and inappropriately attracts some students who are not well suited to the field. The combination means that the decline in quantity of majors is accompanied by a decline in quality as well.

Undergraduate business programs in the mid 1990s still bear a remarkably strong resemblance to business programs in the 1950s, which were developed before computer technology, market globalization, and other forces significantly changed the world in which business is conducted as the twenty-first century approaches. As a reader from Norman, Oklahoma, noted in a letter to the editor in the January 17, 1994 issue of *Business Week,* "It appears most colleges and universities are behind the curve" in adapting to a rapidly changing environment, running the risk that "many universities will be irrelevant to business" (Ellington, 1994, p. 12).

At most colleges, the introductory accounting sequence serves as the portal or gateway to the business school as well as to the accounting major. Thus, the introductory accounting course has the dual responsibility of attracting top-quality accounting majors and providing a strong foundation in accounting and business for all business majors.

The Traditional Approach to Introductory Accounting

What does the traditional introductory accounting sequence look like? For many decades, the format of the sequence has been remarkably homogeneous nationwide. It emphasizes the record-keeping aspects of accounting, focusing on financial accounting record keeping (keeping track of economic transactions that are eventually reported to outsiders in financial statements) and managerial accounting record keeping (keeping track of financial information needed for internal decision making, such as developing product cost information).

The traditional format is procedural, or rules-oriented, in focus. Students are taught the "nuts and bolts" of how to record a variety of economic transactions and how to summarize the recorded information for reporting purposes. As a result, students remember introductory accounting as a "mechanics" class where the key to survival is to learn the rules, such as knowing which accounts to debit and which to credit and always making sure that "debits equal credits." Students come to view accounting as a "one right answer" discipline, where the task is to "crunch the numbers" in a well-structured measurement task.

Although the procedural focus dominates, instructors have long realized that there are other important aspects of accounting that students should be aware of. Thus, there is often some effort also to focus students' attention on the uses of accounting information, the judgmental aspects of accounting, or other important areas of accounting, such as tax, systems, and auditing. Usually, however, relatively little time, compared with the time spent on accounting rules and procedures, is used to cover these topics.

The procedural focus was well suited to the work environment students entered after graduating from business schools in the 1950s, the 1960s, and even the 1970s, when accountants were valued in large part for their ability to get the numbers right. But as the impact of computer technology became significant, the world of accounting changed. Procedural aspects of accounting can be automated and have, by now, been substantially automated. Bar code scanners, electronic data interchange, electronic spreadsheets, relational database programs, expert systems, artificial intelligence programs, and other advances have resulted in a major restructuring of accounting careers. Gone are the rooms full of record keepers, no longer needed in the new environment. Accountants are valued more for their ability to create new kinds of information and to interpret information for use by nonaccountants than for their ability to "crunch the numbers." Getting the numbers right for accountants has become the equivalent of dribbling for an NBA player—a fundamental requirement but not a major determinant of value.

Technological changes also affect users of accounting information (managers, investors, creditors, employees, competitors, government, and others). Users need no longer be restricted to the information available in standard reports. They can now work with accountants to create new measures to suit new information needs. For example, as businesses, governments, and nonprofit organizations began to adopt a Total Quality Management (TQM) philosophy in response to a more competitive environment, accountants worked with managers to help create previously unknown measures to capture the costs of quality. Robert K. Elliott, a partner in the international public accounting firm KPMG Peat Marwick, points out that all these technology-driven changes will inevitably influence educational needs: "Information technology (IT) is changing everything . . . . Obviously, if business, management, and accounting change, accounting education and research must change: the types of students recruited, the curriculum, the set of required capabilities of graduates, and the issues investigated" (Elliott, 1992, p. 61).

By now, the traditional approach to introductory accounting at many institutions may well be a concept kept past its prime. As the Bedford Committee of the American Accounting Association, the primary professional organization for academic accountants, noted in its report *Future Accounting Education: Preparing for the Expanding Profession,* "The accounting profession . . . is in a state of flux, reflecting massive changes taking place in technology and social values, and in social, government, and business institutions" (1986). The committee called for a redirection of accounting education from a perspective that emphasizes its record-keeping functions to one that emphasizes information development for decision-making functions.

In 1989, a coalition of the eight largest accounting firms in the world joined the call for accounting education change. In a white paper entitled *Perspectives on Education: Capabilities for Success in the Accounting Profession,* the firms noted the decline in quantity and quality of accounting majors. They called for a refocusing of accounting courses to stress analytical and conceptual thinking instead of memorization of the voluminous and ever-increasing body of rules accountants apply in their work. The firms also put their money where their mouths were, donating $4 million to establish and fund the Accounting Education Change Commission (AECC), a blue-ribbon commission charged with implementing changes in accounting education. Additional donations were made in 1993 to continue the AECC's work. To date, the AECC has funded curriculum change at approximately a dozen institutions. It is currently conducting a series of efforts to disseminate the results of these projects to other schools. Several of the firms also made individual donations to support other accounting education change projects. For instance, Coopers and Lybrand donated funding to support curriculum revision at the School of Accounting at the University of Southern California (USC). As a result, there is a real movement of change occurring in accounting. As a cover story of *Change: The Magazine of Higher Learning* put it, "Change Where You Might Least Expect It: Accounting Education" (Wyer, 1993).

What Should Be Changed?

The good news is that there is a growing recognition that accounting education needs to change. The bad news is that the degree of change called for is daunting, particularly for the introductory sequence. The new view of accounting education places increased importance on the role of the gateway introductory course and calls for significant changes in both course content and pedagogy.

Increased Recognition of the Importance of Gateway Courses. Society has long recognized the importance of getting off to a good start. Proverbs about the importance of good starts appear in both Plato's (1974) *The Republic* ("The beginning is the most important part of the work" and "The direction in which an education starts a man will determine his future life") and Aristotle's (1962) *Politics* ("Well begun is half done").

Thus it is somewhat surprising that in many academic fields, including accounting and business, introductory courses are often famous for the poor first impressions they create. When asked for their view of an introductory course, students too often remember large sections, dull lectures, contact with teaching assistants rather than professors, impossible tests that have to be curved, lack of involvement, feelings of frustration and high drop rates. In traditional introductory accounting courses, double-digit drop rates are the norm and student impressions are often notoriously negative. For example, one student in the now-defunct traditional introductory accounting sequence at USC described his impression this way, "Accounting is pencil-pushing, pencil-necked geek work. All in all, I'd rather have my wisdom teeth pulled."

One reason for the poor first impression is the relative status of introductory-level undergraduate courses in academia. Introductory accounting has often been given a low priority. "In too many universities (and colleges), . . . at best, departments view the introductory sequence as a chore, necessary and important, but not deserving of special attention or priority resource allocation . . . . At worst, the introductory accounting sequence is seriously neglected; its teaching is foisted off on obsolescent faculty, on part-time instructors or on graduate teaching instructors and minimal funding is assigned" (Manes, 1990, p. 1).

The AECC made particular note of the critical importance of the introductory course in getting students off to a good start and attracting the right majors. It suggested a logical, but significant, redistribution of resources towards the gateway course (Accounting Education Change Commission, 1992). Accountants in practice also recognize the critical importance of the first course in setting the stage for curriculum change. For example, in its 1993 annual report, the KPMG Peat Marwick Foundation notes, "The first-year curriculum presents a unique opportunity for educators to address the expanded role of the accountant in the global marketplace. . . . It is our belief that a modified and enhanced curriculum will serve also to attract students who have traditionally opted for other majors."

Less Rule-Oriented Courses, Broader Context. There is a remarkable degree of consensus among both academics and accounting practitioners about the need to expand the focus of accounting education, internationalize and computerize the curriculum, improve student's analytical and critical thinking skills, and help students form an integrated view of the various aspects of accounting and how they relate to decision making (The Bedford Committee, 1986; *Perspectives* . . . , 1989; Accounting Education Change Commission, 1990). The AECC provides a detailed list of objectives for the first course in accounting, stressing a broad view of accounting's role in society, a broad view of the various aspects of accounting (including tax, auditing and systems, and financial and managerial aspects), a focus on the uses of accounting information, and the development of analytical skills and the ability to confront unstructured problems (Accounting Education Change Committee, 1992).

Whereas the traditional accounting curriculum was notable for its homogeneity, the movement to change accounting education is not resulting in a single uniform curriculum across the country. Different schools have implemented changes in their own ways. However, there are some commonalities. In the August 1993 issue of the *Journal of Accountancy,* Doyle Z. Williams, the first chairman of the AECC, reported on what he saw as the "common ground" in schools undergoing education change, as summarized in the Table 9.1.

A Move to More Interactive Learning. The procedurally oriented traditional introductory accounting course was well suited to the traditional lecture format, where the instructor's job is to impart facts and rules efficiently and the student's job is to absorb them. Thus, it is logical that the primary mode of instructional delivery in the traditional introductory accounting course included lectures and drill and practice homework problems. From the students' point of view, the instructor told you what you needed to know, and you learned it.

However, a change of objectives comes with an accompanying change in pedagogy. To achieve the desired objectives of developing intellectual, communication, and interpersonal skills (in addition to imparting technical knowledge), the learning environment needs to become less teacher-centered and more student-centered. When the focus moves from rules to tools, the instructor's job is not to impart facts and methods but to help students "learn how to learn." The movement to a more interactive learning environment is a

**Table 9.1. A Comparison of Traditional
and New Approaches in Accounting Education**

Traditional	New
Heavy emphasis on technical courses in accounting	Broader emphasis on general education and business and organizational knowledge
Little integration of subject matter—accounting courses taught in isolation	Heavy integration of tax, managerial accounting, financial accounting, systems, and auditing
Heavy emphasis on calculating one right answer	Increased emphasis on solving unstructured problems, such as use of cases
Heavy emphasis on teaching rules	Increased emphasis on the learning process—learning to learn
Heavy emphasis on teaching to the Uniform CPA examination	Recognition of a broader objective
Little attention paid to communication and interpersonal skills	Increased emphasis throughout the accounting curriculum on writing, presentation, and interpersonal skills
Students seen as passive recipients of knowledge	Students seen as active participants in learning
Technology used sparingly in noncomputer courses	Use of technology integrated throughout the accounting curriculum
Introductory accounting focus on preparing external financial reports, journal entries, postings, and so on	Introductory accounting focus on role of accounting in society and in organizations; increased focus of using accounting information for decision making

Source: Williams, 1993. Reprinted with permission from the *Journal of Accountancy.* Copyright 1993 by the American Institute of Certified Public Accountants, Inc. Opinions of the authors are their own and do not necessarily reflect policies of the AICPA.

significant change for accounting educators, and, according to the AECC, should begin in the gateway introductory course (Accounting Education Change Commission, 1992).

Changing Introductory Accounting: The USC Experience

USC was one of the pioneers of the accounting education change movement. The School of Accounting at USC began its "Year 2000" Curriculum Project in January 1987, well before the AECC was formed. The school's comprehensive revision of the undergraduate accounting curriculum began with a new year-long (two-semester) introductory course for sophomores, Core Concepts of Accounting Information, which was first offered in 1991. New courses at the junior and senior level were introduced in 1992 and 1993, with the first class of new curriculum students graduating in December 1993. (For a detailed description of the new curriculum, including course syllabi, see Diamond and Pincus, 1994.)

The Core Concepts of Accounting Information Course. Core Concepts of Accounting Information is such a departure from the traditional introductory course that new materials had to be developed and new instructor training and support systems had to be instituted. The course materials are written in a modular fashion to simplify updating and provide increased flexibility. The course itself is organized into eighteen modules covering four "themes": the users/uses of accounting information; accounting issues involving income and cash flows; accounting issues involving economic resources; and accounting issues involving capital (Pincus, 1993a, 1993b, 1993c, 1993d). A series of outside speakers have helped faculty prepare for a change in pedagogy. To provide continuing support, an instruction team approach was established where all course instructors meet on a regular basis to discuss pedagogical successes and problems.

The key features of the course are very much in keeping with the AECC recommendations issued a year and a half after the course began. Some of the key features of the course are the following (Pincus, 1993e).

A focus on the user, not the preparer, and on concepts and tools, rather than rules. To accomplish this focus, the structure of the course is built around user groups. The first module in each theme is an introduction, providing an overview of the concepts and issues to be covered and the appropriate terminology. In keeping with the user orientation, the remaining modules address the information needs of each major user group—management, owners and creditors, government, and so on. Accounting topics are introduced as they relate to a particular user group, using the example of a real organization. For instance, financial accounting for inventory is introduced as it is used by Mattel Corporation.

An integrated approach to accounting education, introducing basic concepts and issues across all the functional areas of accounting, including systems, tax and auditing, and financial and management accounting. The integrated approach gives students a better understanding of the scope of the accounting profession and the nature of accounting careers. For example, the section on inventory not only covers recording inventory transactions for financial statements and developing product costs for internal decision making but also discusses how information systems affect the ability to produce different measurements, how different users have different information needs about inventory, how taxes affect inventory decisions, and how to audit inventory.

An accent on contemporary examples involving international and domestic businesses, and nonprofit and government organizations. Course materials are revised annually to keep the examples current so that students can see connections between the topics they are covering in class and those they are reading about in the financial press or hearing about on news broadcasts. For example, the 1993 edition included an assignment on President Clinton's tax proposals. The international focus can be seen in coverage of international, as well as domestic, accounting standards, and tax issues. For example, in the section on inventory accounting, international accounting standards are the initial focus of discussion, with domestic accounting standards introduced afterward. Government issues covered include the role accounting can play in improving government budgets and controlling deficits and public debt, and accounting issues in government contracts.

An emphasis on skills development as well as technical accounting knowledge, including group assignments, written and oral presentations, electronic research assignments, and ethics and values assignments. Each theme contains assignments suitable for individual and group work as well as a variety of assignments that allow written responses and oral presentations. Ethics assignments are found in every theme. These assignments are integrated into the coverage of the topic, enhancing the students' understanding of the importance of ethics. As an additional resource, supplementary material is provided throughout the first theme to help students build basic skills in working in groups, making oral presentations, and presenting accounting information graphically.

Course material that supports a change to an interactive learning environment. As part of the attempt to create an interactive classroom, course materials are designed to be read by the student, not lectured on. A text of conversational tone supplemented with many illustrations and examples makes the materials accessible to students. Instructor materials suggest ways to approach classroom discussion of unstructured problems, provide background readings to spark ideas, and offer guidelines for evaluating student responses to assignments that do not have "one right answer."

Benefits and Outcomes

From 1991 through 1993, over thirty-five hundred students took the new introductory sequence and over two dozen people taught the course, including full-time and part-time faculty, doctoral students, retired practitioner "executives in residence," an international visiting professor, and a local community college instructor interested in accounting education change. As with any major change, transition costs—particularly in the short-run—are high for administrators, students, and faculty. (See Mock, Pincus, and Andre, 1991, and Diamond and Pincus, 1994, for a discussion of transition costs.) But the costs decrease with time while the benefits accumulate. Although it is still too early to report comprehensive assessment results, some of the early performance indicators for the new approach to introductory accounting can be reported. For example (Pincus, 1993e):

Enrollment Increases. Each year the new introductory sequence has been offered, course enrollment has increased. This is a particularly important indicator. Enrollment at the university has not increased during this period and the number of incoming students indicating an early intent to major in business or accounting has actually decreased. Moreover, the enrollment increase means that many "new" audiences for accounting are being reached. Groups of students who did not tend to take the traditional introductory financial and managerial accounting courses are now enrolling in the introductory sequence. For example, the new course attracts political science students because of its discussion of governments. This is an important indicator because the expanded audience provides an opportunity to educate more people about the role of accounting in society and provides a new pool of potential majors.

Increased Interest in the Major. Applications to be admitted to the School of Accounting as accounting majors have increased over the first three years of the new curriculum.

Changes in Students Attracted to the Major. The quantity of applications is up and there are some signs that different types of students are applying. For example, junior year instructors note a marked difference in the intellectual aggressiveness of their students. Further, although many students who indicated an early intention to major in accounting do apply, some students who were initially attracted to accounting because of a precollege (that is, high school) bookkeeping course have changed their minds.

Positive Feedback. Both upper-division faculty and employers of student interns have noted a significant improvement in group skills and communication skills. Employers, in particular, have noted a greater awareness of business issues.

Reduced Drop Rates. Even though the course has a reputation for tough—some students say impossible—grading standards, the drop rate for the new introductory sequence has consistently been below 3 percent, far below the drop rate for the traditional introductory sequence. Faculty attribute the significant decline to increased student interest and motivation resulting from the interactive learning environment. Students are involved in the classroom on a daily basis, which offers them increased motivation to keep up with the work. The group work too helps motivate students and creates a support system for learning.

The changes occurring in accounting education echo themes heard throughout academe. In looking back at USC's "Year 2000" curriculum project, I am struck most by the fact that change is a growth process for students and faculty alike. Although change is never easy, progress requires change. As President Kennedy noted in a 1963 speech in Frankfurt, Germany: "Change is the law of life. And those who look only to the past or the present are certain to miss the future."

References

Accounting Education Change Commission. "Position Statement No. One: Objectives of Education for Accountants." *Issues in Accounting Education,* Fall 1990, pp. 306–312.

Accounting Education Change Commission. "Position Statement No. Two: The First Course in Accounting." *Issues in Accounting Education*, Fall 1992, pp. 249–252.

Aristotle. *The Politics*. (T. A. Sinclair, trans.) Baltimore, Md.: Penguin Books, 1962.

Bedford Committee, The (Committee on the Future Content, Structure and Scope of Accounting Education, American Accounting Association). "Future Accounting Education: Preparing for the Expanded Profession." *Issues in Accounting Education*, Spring 1986, pp. 169–190.

Diamond, M. A., and Pincus, K. V. *The USC Year 2000 Curriculum Project*. New York: Coopers and Lybrand Foundation, 1994.

Ellington, R. T. Untitled letter to the editor. *Business Week*, Jan. 17, 1994, p. 12.

Elliott, R. K. "The Third Wave Breaks on the Shores of Accounting." *Accounting Horizons*, June 1992, pp. 61–85.

KPMG Peat Marwick Foundation. *1993 Annual Report*. New York: KPMG Peat Marwick, 1993.

Manes, R. "The Right Start." Florida State University working paper presented at the symposium on models in accounting education, Dallas, Texas, Mar. 8–9, 1990.

Mock, T. J., Pincus, K. V., and Andre, J. M. "A Systems Approach to Accounting Curriculum Development." *Issues in Accounting Education*, Fall 1991, pp. 178–192.

Perspectives on Education: Capabilities for Success in the Accounting Profession. New York: Arthur Andersen & Co., Arthur Young, Coopers and Lybrand, Deloitte Haskins & Sells, Ernst & Whinney, Peat Marwick Main & Co., Price Waterhouse, and Touche Ross, 1989.

Pincus, K. V. *Core Concepts of Accounting Information Theme I—The Users/Uses of Accounting Information*. New York: McGraw-Hill, 1993a.

Pincus, K. V. *Core Concepts of Accounting Information Theme II—Accounting Issues Involving Income and Cash Flows*. New York: McGraw-Hill, 1993b.

Pincus, K. V. *Core Concepts of Accounting Information Theme III—Accounting Issues Involving Economic Resources*. New York: McGraw-Hill, 1993c.

Pincus, K. V. *Core Concepts of Accounting Information Theme IV—Accounting Issues Involving Capital*. New York: McGraw-Hill, 1993d.

Pincus, K. V. *Core Concepts of Accounting Information: Planning Guide for Course Instructors*. New York: McGraw-Hill, 1993e.

Plato. *The Republic*. (G.M.A. Grobe, trans.) Indianapolis, Ind.: Hackett, 1974.

Williams, D. Z. "Reforming Accounting Education." *Journal of Accountancy*, Aug. 1993, pp. 76–82.

Wyer, J. C. "Change Where You Might Least Expect It: Accounting Education." *Change*, Jan./Feb. 1993, pp. 12–17.

KAREN V. PINCUS is associate professor of accounting at the University of Southern California. The Core Concepts of Accounting Information course materials were named the 1992 winner of the American Accounting Association's Innovation in Accounting Education Award.

A statistics course that incorporates seven characteristics of active learning is reenvisioned as a "cognitive apprenticeship" in which students use statistics to address authentic dilemmas of professional practice.

Reenvisioning Statistics: A Cognitive Apprenticeship Approach

Eleanor W. Willemsen, Joanne Gainen

In our work together on this book, we have discerned seven clearly identifiable characteristics in the courses described: experiential learning, collaboration, discovery, use of authentic problems, planning before doing, risk taking, and integrative learning. At first we thought we could describe these innovative courses in terms of these characteristics. However, we found that they alone did not capture the cultural transformation we experienced vicariously through the course descriptions in this volume. This transformation, in our view, amounts to a new paradigm or way of thinking about teaching and learning.

In this chapter, we begin by briefly illustrating the seven characteristics. We then introduce the metaphor of "cognitive apprenticeship" (Collins, Brown, and Newman, 1989) to explain more fully the culture of teaching and learning that emerges when these principles interact. We conclude by describing Willemsen's course for psychology students learning statistics (described in Chapter Two), redesigned as a cognitive apprenticeship.

Seven Characteristics of Active Learning

In this section, we illustrate each of the seven characteristics through its application in one of the courses described in this volume and in Willemsen's statistics course.

Experiential Learning. In experiential learning programs, students *do* rather than merely *learn about* the work of a discipline. In the workshop physics course described by Laws, Rosborough, and Poodry (Chapter Eight), for example, firsthand experiences with microcomputer-based laboratory materials help students build conceptual understanding of physics and develop investigative skills. In Willemsen's statistics course, students select data from a data base and analyze it on computers using a simplified statistical software package.

Collaboration. Collaborative learning is a central feature of the calculus workshop described by Bonsangue and Drew (Chapter Three), where minority students work in groups to solve challenging problems. In Willemsen's statistics course, students also work in collaborative groups all term.

Discovery. In laboratory experiences in discovery chemistry described by Ditzler and Ricci (Chapter Four) students discover fundamental aspects of the discipline using a pool of class-generated data. In Willemsen's statistics, students "discover" the standard deviation, level of significance, and sampling error.

Use of Authentic Problems. The use of authentic problems is most evident in the EPICS program described by Pavelich, Olds, and Miller (Chapter Five), where teams of engineering and science students interact with agencies to solve agency-generated problems. The self-referent data used in Willemsen's statistics course offers opportunities to address questions typical of those asked by researchers studying individual differences.

Planning Before Doing. Planning, an important metacognitive skill, is most explicitly addressed in Troeger's computer science course (Chapter Six). Students analyze problems and develop a "design idea" before they begin writing code. In Willemsen's statistics course, planning is most evident in the group work on the two miniature research reports.

Risk Taking. In the graphics course described by Sanchez, Hight, and Gainen (Chapter Seven), students learn to overcome the "fear of sketching" that inhibits their use of this essential design tool. Similarly, in Willemsen's statistics course, students must transform questions of interest into problems that can be solved with textbook tools.

Integrative Learning. Integrative learning is evident in the "Year 2000" accounting curriculum described by Pincus (Chapter Nine), in which students learn to analyze business functions such as inventory from the perspective of the five functional areas of accounting. Similarly, minireports in Willemsen's statistics course require integration of all of the steps involved in psychological research.

Limitations

These characteristics create a valuable checklist of good practice for active learning in introductory quantitative courses. As the preceding paragraphs indicate, analysis of Willemsen's statistics course in terms of these principles reveals that there was a good match. Further, the active learning approach was well received by students. On a follow-up questionnaire, nearly all students who had taken the course agreed that it had increased their level of comfort with statistics, suggesting success in fostering "I can do it" metacognitions. Most students also agreed that they had acquired a good understanding of concepts introduced in the course. Ratings as well as comments suggested that students would welcome even more time spent in group work.

Nonetheless, as noted in Chapter Two, students did not always engage the subject of the course at the level we would have liked. The professor was disappointed that, after the first few weeks, she once again began to hear the familiar refrain, "It's so much clearer when you explain it." Survey results substantiated the fact that students continued to wish for procedural learning: they gave the six-step hypothesis testing model a score of 4.7 on a five-point scale, higher than any other feature of the course. The self-referent data base became just another set of numbers, and collaboration, although popular with the students, was sometimes undermined when a single vocal student dominated the group. Although students enjoyed the course more and performed well in it on the whole, it would be rewarding to move students toward greater independence and involvement.

Thus, in attempting to apply the principles discretely to this course, we found that we could incorporate the principles without generating the level of student involvement reflected in the accounts by other authors included in this monograph. Searching for a way to integrate and transcend the principles, we found that "cognitive apprenticeship" (Collins, Brown, and Newman, 1989) helped us to think about the course as more than a collection of active learning strategies. This model uses the metaphor of apprentices learning a craft, rather than students learning a subject, to understand the development of expert practice. After briefly explaining cognitive apprenticeship, we describe how it has changed our thinking about the statistics course.

Cognitive Apprenticeship

The concept of cognitive apprenticeship derives from the observation that "just plain folks" (JPFs) often learn through enculturation into a community as well as through formal instruction (Brown, Collins, and Duguid, 1989). Task-oriented, everyday situations are a rich source of learning in which people become part of a community by observing, practicing, and getting help with the activities of that community. Many young people, for instance, learn to fix cars by helping to repair and maintain an older sibling's vehicle. Friends teach each other the latest popular dances or how to use a new software package. Understanding of the skill develops through activity involving the tools, materials, and language of the community in situations similar to or identical with those in which it is used. This contextualized understanding is referred to as "situated cognition" (Brown, Collins, and Duguid, 1989).

The metaphor of apprentice-learning-a-craft is illustrated in the anthropological literature by tailors' shops in Liberia, where apprentices learn from masters and the more advanced apprentices produce and sell garments. Apprentices alternate between observation of the master and attempts to duplicate the master's performance of a whole task. They begin by performing simple, low-risk, but conceptually important tasks, such as ironing or hemming cuffs, and advance to tasks that involve more responsibility and risk, such as sewing a garment or cutting fabric. The more skilled the apprentice becomes, the higher the price he can command for his work, so his efforts and accomplishments have intrinsic value (Lave, 1988).

The cognitive apprenticeship model described by Collins, Brown, and Newman presents three features: authentic activity, cognitive scaffolding, and expert practice (Brown, Collins, and Duguid, 1989; Collins, Brown, and Newman, 1989).

Authentic Activity. The learner's participation in "authentic" activity, defined as "the ordinary practices of the culture" (Brown, Collins, and Duguid, 1989, p. 34), is the first feature of cognitive apprenticeship. Cognitive apprenticeship engages learners in tasks that approximate what a practitioner in the field actually does. Students become intrigued by the opportunity to solve genuine problems, a more intrinsically motivating task than memorizing information or following the academic equivalent of a recipe in the laboratory. Authentic activity and situated cognition are evident in each of the seven curricula presented in this monograph, particularly the client-based team problem-solving model described by Pavelich, Olds, and Miller (Chapter Five).

Cognitive Scaffolding. Cognitive scaffolding, the second feature of the apprenticeship model, is a concept borrowed from Vygotsky (1978). Scaffolding refers to features of the instructional situation that let the learner accomplish as much of the task as possible on her own while making available the support she needs to reach a level beyond her immediate grasp. Cognitive scaffolding includes modeling the targeted task, coaching, and encouraging increasingly independent performance by gradually reducing or "fading" these supports as the learner's skill increases. Scaffolding provides occasions for both master and apprentice to verbalize normally covert cognitive and metacognitive processes, thus helping the apprentice develop metacognitive skills such as self-monitoring and self-correction (Collins, Brown, and Newman, 1989). Scaffolding is perhaps most evident in the graphic engineering course described by Sanchez, Hight, and Gainen (Chapter Seven), particularly when students review and evaluate the posters of students from earlier classes, generating criteria for evaluation of their own work.

Expert Practice. The third feature is the creation of a "culture of expert practice," defined as "a learning environment in which the participants actively communicate about and engage in the skills involved in expertise, where expertise is understood as the practice of solving problems and carrying out tasks in a domain" (Collins, Brown, and Newman, 1989, p. 488). In contrast to the instructor-centered environment of most classrooms, the activity, which approximates the work of practitioners, is central here (Brown, Collins, and Duguid, 1989). In this culture, students observe and assist each other, guided by the professor or an advanced undergraduate facilitator (as in programs described by Bonsangue and Drew in Chapter Three and by Troeger in Chapter Six). They may even engage in friendly competition of the sort that energizes the work of many scholars and researchers, furthering their socialization into the culture of expert practice. Ditzler and Ricci (Chapter Four) exemplify the culture of expert practice in their commitment to let students "learn chemistry as chemists do it."

Application of the Cognitive Apprenticeship Model in Elementary Statistics

To integrate and apply the diverse ideas presented in this volume, we have redesigned the statistics course described in Chapter Two using the cognitive apprentice model. This model helped us to make a paradigm shift from instructor-directed active learning to cognitive apprenticeship. Our working title for this new statistics course is the "Reenvisioned Elementary Statistics Course Used by Eleanor" (RESCUE). RESCUE embeds traditional course content within realistic practitioner dilemmas, introducing statistical concepts and methods as tools to respond to these dilemmas.

Goals of RESCUE. To define RESCUE's goals, we began by redefining the goals of the statistics course to reflect both the realities of practice and the interests of the students taking the course. Most students majoring in psychology aspire to careers in counseling in clinical mental health or school settings. They do not see themselves as future researchers. Many would prefer not to take statistics at all. Given the choice between anecdotal evidence and statistical data, many would rely on the anecdotal. Few recognize that clinical practitioners are consumers of statistical information and may be called upon to use statistical methods in the social service settings they work in. The cognitive apprenticeship model suggests to us that the redesigned statistics course should enable students to (a) develop a mental model of statistics as a useful tool for practitioners in social service settings, (b) feel comfortable adapting and presenting statistical information for a variety of audiences and purposes, and (c) use statistics as a means to evaluate the relative worth of often conflicting research-based advice. Moreover, it should be taught in a manner that enables students to draw on the strengths of their personal and cultural backgrounds and to discover continuities between their present and future (professional) identities.

Authentic Activity. To accomplish these goals, we will establish a context for authentic problem solving by immersing students in a simulated practice situation. The course will be organized around the activities of a hypothetical middle school that has been designated a "magnet school," that is, a school with special curriculum designed to attract families in districts undergoing court-ordered desegregation. Because it is a magnet school, the faculty, administration, and counseling staff frequently engage in applied research related to experimental programs, funding requests, and challenges to their underlying philosophy. The staff will thus face a series of dilemmas that will be presented as scenarios involving questions or decisions of real concern to the school. Working in teams, the students will take on staff roles and develop responses to each of the scenarios. Each scenario will culminate in presentation of the teams' findings to an appropriate hypothetical audience, either orally, graphically, in writing, or in combination.

Expert Practice. For each scenario, teams will act as experts: they will select and analyze relevant data from a data base that includes information about students' ethnicity, gender, family income, family size and family structure, grades, attitudes, self-perception measures, parent and teacher perceptions, and approximately twenty other scores, for each of three hundred students. The data set will also include measures of teacher satisfaction, beliefs, and attitudes; ratings of public confidence; and information about students in several previous cohorts. The textbook and handouts will serve as the resources for students to use to respond to the problems of this hypothetical school. Discussion of approaches to each scenario will offer opportunities to introduce heuristics of statistical inquiry and usage in a social context.

Cognitive Scaffolding. The cognitive and social challenges of this course will require considerable scaffolding. RESCUE will ask students to translate a broad question or dilemma into the more familiar form of a problem requiring a particular set of data and mode of presentation. Scaffolding will be needed to help them learn to approach ill-defined problems. The course will therefore include explicit modeling and coaching of problem-solving strategies so that students develop metacognitive awareness of the activity. The professor may introduce a model of the problem-solving process (such as Schoenfeld, 1985, chap. 9) and then emphasize a particular aspect of the process in conjunction with each scenario. For example, identifying broad goals and generating subgoals within them might be introduced as a planning strategy in the first scenario. Exploring the problem by recalling relevant concepts could be introduced when addressing scenarios that would require students to choose between several possible statistical tools, and so on.

The students will have to imagine themselves in practitioner roles (administrators, teachers, counselors, parents, board members) with which they may be only moderately familiar, and they will have to work effectively with teammates to develop and present a satisfactory response to each scenario. For the role-play, the scaffolding may involve a brainstorming session in which students consider the perspectives of each group or individual and how the presentation can speak directly and forcefully to them. Teamwork, too, will require scaffolding. Instruction should therefore include discussion of specific teamwork skills, including setting goals, taking turns, considering different perspectives, assigning tasks, and summing up results. To ensure an inclusive environment, the class should generate a set of ground rules for small-group work and class discussion.

Content and Methods of the Redesigned Statistics Course

This section outlines how several important topics in the traditional introductory statistics course will be handled in the RESCUE model. For each topic, we begin with the scenario that we will present to the students and then identify the concept, method, or skill (cognitive, metacognitive, or social) that it will introduce.

Visual Display of Data to Persuade an Audience. In the first scenario of the course, each group will be asked to imagine that they are a team of reading teachers appealing to a United Way committee for funding of a computer-based reading laboratory. The goal will be to prepare a 10-minute presentation that will convince the committee that their school needs and deserves funding. Data will be available for ten classrooms. Groups will select the data they wish to present and prepare their displays—perhaps as posters—for presentation to other class members. Following each presentation, the class will discuss how the group approached the task, why they chose that approach, the strengths of the presentation, and the unanswered questions. At this point the professor might use the displays as the basis for an integrative discussion of data presentation techniques. The scenario could conclude with a brief discussion of strategies used by each group to achieve their goals.

Through this simple but meaningful task, students will begin to develop an essential skill: how to present a set of data in a form an audience can easily understand. They will also learn how to think about the problem of presenting data to a (potentially resistant) audience and will generate criteria they will be able to use to guide their own future presentations. Their first success working as a group on a statistical problem should help them develop confidence in their abilities and trust in their teammates, thus building a foundation for future collaboration and persistence in the face of more difficult assignments.

Conveying School Performance: Central Tendencies and Variability. In the next scenario, we will ask each group to think of itself as a committee of faculty who have been asked to let a liaison officer in the State Education Office know how the school is doing "overall in the six 'basic' subjects." A two-page letter with tables has been requested (the officer is busy), they will be told. Students will find that the graphs and charts they learned to create in the first scenario are useful for a visual overview of one or two variables but quickly become cumbersome when information on many variables must be conveyed. For this assignment, then, students will find that the mean and standard deviation offer a concise, informative way to respond to the state officer's request. With help from the textbook and coaching by the professor, they will learn both the value of these simple descriptive statistics and the method for obtaining them. As part of the evaluation, teams might play the role of the state officer responding to one or more of the presentations with praise, concerns, or a request for further information.

Determining Individual Student Subjects' Characteristics and Needs. Teachers and counselors must develop an "individual educational plan" (IEP) for children who have have or are suspected of having a disability, no matter what kind, that would make it difficult for them to be adequately educated in the school's regular classroom programs. IEPs are usually drawn up during one or more conferences involving the child's teacher, various "experts" (psychologist, speech therapist, social worker, reading specialist, and so on), the parent, and any special advocate the family wishes to involve. Developing an IEP requires understanding how children compare with their groups; it also requires a "profile" of the learners' characteristics to determine relative strengths and weaknesses in cognitive, social, and physical abilities.

Each group in the RESCUE statistics course will be assigned to develop an IEP for a child in the school's data base. Students will convey this information for their group's child in a report using the standard score—or z-score—to describe how an individual child compares with other children and to standardize the child's performance on a variety of measures that would otherwise be difficult to compare.

Identifying Predictive Factors for Program Design/Development. Attitudes toward school in the middle school years is an important predictor of dropouts later on. Acting as teachers concerned about high drop-out rates, the students will seek to convince the principal that letting them research relationships among attitudes toward school and other variables associated with dropping out is a worthwhile and feasible task. As each group presents its rationale, class members may play the roles of skeptical administrators, politically sensitive board members, and parents who do not want any teacher time "wasted."

Explaining the benefits of conducting the necessary analyses, students will develop their understanding of correlation and regression. By finding the correlates of attitude toward school, students will also come to appreciate the power of correlation and regression and how these methods work. The students will complete the scenario by communicating in their report to the principle some ideas of their own, derived from their investigations.

Discriminatory Treatment? Applying Probabilistic Reasoning. In this scenario, a group of angry parents confronts the principal with charges of sex discrimination in the school, claiming that several teachers unfairly target boys in complaints of "problem behavior." The students will be asked to serve as consultants who will prepare a report for a team sent from the federal Office of Equal Opportunity to investigate. To address this issue, students will need to use concepts of probability. They will eventually need to frame the question, "How likely is it that the observed pattern of problem reporting could have occurred by chance?"

We expect that students will approach the task by using their now-honed data presentation skills to prepare simple tables (or their conceptual equivalents) showing the number of boys and the number of girls that were the subject of "teacher complaints about problem behaviors" during the year. We expect them to realize that to interpret correctly the number of complaints for each sex, they will have to consider frequency counts for boys and girls who do not receive teacher complaints so that they can determine the rate of complaints for the two sexes. Having done this, they will attempt to decide whether gender discrimination has occurred and to justify their position. The discussion should prove controversial, because most teams will not have established criteria for determining whether the rate for one sex is significantly different from the rate for the other.

At this point, the concept of hypothesis testing could be meaningfully introduced. After a brief explanation of the concept of hypothesis testing, each group will be asked to formulate its position in terms of the null hypothesis and its alternative. The groups will then be asked to consider how they might decide which hypothesis is correct. In the ensuing discussion, students will be asked to identify all the factors that might make it difficult to do so. Although they may not use terms such as *sampling error* or *level of significance,* we expect that they will describe the concepts that underlie these terms. The terminology can then be meaningfully introduced. In short, by asking students to solve a problem of *educational practice* (investigating parental complaints), they will generate a subproblem of *statistical practice* (learning how to determine which hypothesis the data support).

A great deal of scaffolding may be necessary to help the students clarify their hypotheses, select the appropriate statistics, develop criteria for rejection or acceptance of the null hypothesis, and test their results. Having been through the process once, however, they should be ready to review what they have done and to articulate in more formal terms what began as an intuitive approach drawing on previously learned concepts and methods. The discussion at this point will be pivotal: it should guide students to articulate a framework for hypothesis testing, including the key ideas of null and alternative hypotheses, sampling error, level of significance, and so on. The professor will invite students to compare this approach with their intuitive judgments, and consider how it might be applied in a variety of practice situations. Finally, the professor will encourage students to evaluate the assumptions that make statistical inference the dominant paradigm for scientific inquiry today (Project Kaleideoscope, 1991).

The goal of this scenario and ensuing discussion is to help students construct a conceptual model that approximates an expert practitioner's understanding of probability and its relationship to hypothesis testing. This approximation will continue to be refined as students put it into practice in their attempts to resolve additional scenarios and master the remaining concepts of the course.

Additional Scenarios. Additional scenarios will include a challenge from the local school board suggesting that the school is not "doing its job" in mathematics and science preparation (requiring analysis of data from standardized tests using known population parameters) and a counterargument that students are developing important abilities not tested by standardized tests (requiring analysis of data from locally developed measures and leading to consideration of the need to estimate the standard deviation of these scores with resulting changes in the model of probability used to evaluate results). A final scenario will involve the use of change scores and group comparisons to demonstrate effects of the computerized reading lab that was funded as a result of students' presentations in the first scenario of the course.

Cognitive Apprenticeship Revisited

The cognitive apprenticeship model helped us begin to articulate a paradigm shift from instructor-directed active learning to a qualitatively different conception involving students as apprentices to faculty active learners. We recognize that we have only sketched the outlines of our rethinking, and that implementing these ideas will call upon all of our resources as teachers, practitioners, and cognitive-social psychologists to overcome students' insecurity about tackling ill-defined problems. We also expect many of our colleagues in psychology to greet our proposal with skepticism. We are willing to test and evaluate our results. We believe the outcome will be a qualitatively different classroom culture that motivates students by engaging them in challenging activity that has relevance to their career goals and supports them with generous scaffolding to help them develop a sense of efficacy—the "I can do it" attitude valued by the professor. The RESCUE model will allow students to gain this attitude as they discover for themselves the value of statistical competence. Finally, the course will transport statistics from the realm of abstract science, which is unfamiliar and uninviting to people-oriented psychology majors, into the realm of everyday professional practice, which the students can identify with.

References

Brown, J. S., Collins, A., and Duguid, P. "Situated Cognition and the Culture of Learning." *Educational Researcher,* Jan./Feb. 1989, pp. 32–42.

Collins, A., Brown, J. S., and Newman, S. E. "Cognitive Apprenticeship: Teaching the Craft of Reading, Writing, and Mathematics." In L. B. Resnick (ed.), *Knowing, Learning, and Instruction: Essays in Honor of Robert Glaser.* Hillsdale, N.J.: Erlbaum, 1989.

Lave, J. *The Culture of Acquisition and the Practice of Understanding.* Report no. IRL88–0007. Palo Alto, Calif.: Institute for Research on Learning, May 1988.

Project Kaleidoscope. *What Works: Building Natural Science Communities: A Plan for Strengthening Undergraduate Science and Mathematics.* Vol. 1. Washington, D.C.: The Independent Colleges Office, 1991.

Schoenfeld, A. H. *Mathematical Problem Solving.* New York: Academic Press, 1985.

Vygotsky, L. *Mind in Society: The Development of Higher Psychological Processes.* Cambridge, Mass.: Harvard University Press, 1978.

ELEANOR W. WILLEMSEN *is associate professor of psychology at Santa Clara University, where she teaches statistics and developmental psychology. She conducts research on attachment and serves as an advocate for children in the foster care system.*

JOANNE GAINEN *directs the Teaching and Learning Center at Santa Clara University, where she is working with faculty who teach quantitative courses to develop peer-facilitated group study programs.*

INDEX

Academic Excellence Workshop (AEW) program (Cal Poly), 24, 26; cost of, 31; facilitator role in, 26, 30–31; and gender/minority issues, 30; minority student involvement in, 24–25; and nonworkshop minority students, 27–28; and precollege achievement, 27; and skimming/self-selection, 29; structure of, 25–26; student experiences in, 30; study, 24–32; and white/Asian American students, 25, 28–29

Accounting courses: broader context of, 93; impersonalness of, 11–12; importance of introductory, 92–93; and interactive learning, 93–94; and mathematics ability, 6; procedural focus of, 90–91; technological impact on, 90–91; traditional approach to, 90–92. *See also* Core Concepts of Accounting Information course (University of Southern California)

Accounting Education Change Commission (AECC), 91–94, 99

Activity-based learning, 77–78, 86

African Americans: and AEW study, 24–25; Emerging Scholars Program for, 23–24; improving persistence in SME of, 9; precollege preparation of, 6; study practices of, 8–9. *See also* Minority students; Students of color

Algorithms, and computer science, 57

American Association of Collegiate Schools of Business, 89

American Council on Education, 89

American Mathematical Association of Two Year Colleges (AMATYC), 23

American Mathematical Society, 23

Andre, J. M., 97

Aristotle, 92

Arnold, K., 10

Asian Americans, and Academic Excellence Workshop program, 25, 28–29

Astin, A., 7

Attrition: and aptitude, 5; and classroom climate, 9–11; and course culture, 11–13; and gateway courses, 1–2, 5; and instructional culture, 11–12; and

peer culture, 7–9; and peer group interaction, 8; and precollege educational experiences, 6–7; in SME courses, 1, 5–13; of students of color, 1, 5–13

Authentic activity, 102–104

Bandura, A., 17

Bedford Committee, The, 91, 93

Belenky, M., 2, 19, 69, 78, 85, 86

Blanc, R. A., 9

Bloom, G., 65

Bonsangue, M. V., 9, 10, 13, 25, 29, 30, 31

Bradsford, J. D., 22

Brown, A. L., 22

Brown, J. S., 3, 99, 101, 102

Brush, S. G., 6, 10, 11

Bull, R., 46

Business courses/majors: as "behind the curve," 90; enrollment drop in, 89; and minority students, 89. *See also* Accounting courses

Calculus courses: Academic Excellence Workshop model of (study), 24–32; Emerging Scholars Program model for, 23–24

Calculus-based physics courses. *See* Workshop physics project (Dickinson College)

California State Polytechnic University, Pomona (Cal Poly), 24

Campione, J. C., 22

Carmichael, J. W., 7

Carpenter, V. L., 5

CHALLENGE transition program (Georgia Institute of Technology), 7

Chemistry courses: at College of Holy Cross, 35–43; discovery approach to, 35–36; guided-inquiry format for teaching, 36–37; model for laboratory-based, 37–39; students view of, 35. *See also* Discovery chemistry

Chinese Americans, study practices of, 8–9. *See also* Asian Americans; Minority students; Students of color

City College of New York (CCNY), 55

109

ORDERING INFORMATION

NEW DIRECTIONS FOR TEACHING AND LEARNING is a series of paperback books that presents ideas and techniques for improving college teaching, based both on the practical expertise of seasoned instructors and on the latest research findings of educational and psychological researchers. Books in the series are published quarterly in spring, summer, fall, and winter and are available for purchase by subscription as well as by single copy.

SUBSCRIPTIONS for 1995 cost $48.00 for individuals (a savings of 25 percent over single-copy prices) and $64.00 for institutions, agencies, and libraries. Please do not send institutional checks for personal subscriptions. Standing orders are accepted.

SINGLE COPIES cost $15.95 when payment accompanies order. (California, New Jersey, New York, and Washington, D.C., residents please include appropriate sales tax.) Billed orders will be charged postage and handling.

DISCOUNTS FOR QUANTITY ORDERS are available. Please write to the address below for information.

ALL ORDERS must include either the name of an individual or an official purchase order number. Please submit your order as follows:
    Subscriptions: specify series and year subscription is to begin
    Single copies: include individual title code (such as TL54)

MAIL ALL ORDERS TO:
    Jossey-Bass Publishers
    350 Sansome Street
    San Francisco, CA 94104-1342

FOR SUBSCRIPTION SALES OUTSIDE OF THE UNITED STATES, CONTACT:
    any international subscription agency or Jossey-Bass directly.

OTHER TITLES AVAILABLE IN THE
NEW DIRECTIONS FOR TEACHING AND LEARNING SERIES
Robert J. Menges, Editor-in-Chief
Marilla D. Svinicki, Associate Editor

TL60   Supplemental Instruction: Increasing Achievement and Retention, *Deanna C. Martin, David R. Arendale*

TL59   Collaborative Learning: Underlying Processes and Effective Techniques, *Kris Bosworth, Sharon J. Hamilton*

TL58   Interdisciplinary Studies Today, *Julie Thompson Klein, William G. Doty*

TL57   Mentoring Revisited: Making an Impact on Individuals and Institutions, *Marie A. Wunsch*

TL56   Student Self-Evaluation: Fostering Reflective Learning, *Jean MacGregor*

TL55   Developing Senior Faculty as Teachers, *Martin J. Finkelstein, Mark W. LaCelle-Peterson*

TL54   Preparing Faculty for the New Conceptions of Scholarship, *Laurie Richlin*

TL53   Building a Diverse Faculty, *Joanne Gainen, Robert Boice*

TL52   Promoting Diversity in College Classrooms: Innovative Responses for the Curriculum, Faculty, and Institutions, *Maurianne Adams*

TL51   Teaching in the Information Age: The Role of Educational Technology, *Michael J. Albright, David L. Graf*

TL50   Developing New and Junior Faculty, *Mary Deane Sorcinelli, Ann E. Austin*

TL49   Teaching for Diversity, *Laura L. B. Border, Nancy Van Note Chism*

TL48   Effective Practices for Improving Teaching, *Michael Theall, Jennifer Franklin*

TL47   Applying the Seven Principles for Good Practice in Undergraduate Education, *Arthur W. Chickering, Zelda F. Gamson*

TL46   Classroom Research: Early Lessons from Success, *Thomas A. Angelo*

TL45   College Teaching: From Theory to Practice, *Robert J. Menges, Marilla D. Svinicki*

TL44   Excellent Teaching in a Changing Academy: Essays in Honor of Kenneth Eble, *Feroza Jussawalla*

TL43   Student Ratings of Instruction: Issues for Improving Practice, *Michael Theall, Jennifer Franklin*

TL42   The Changing Face of College Teaching, *Marilla D. Svinicki*

TL41   Learning Communities: Creating Connections Among Students, Faculty, and Disciplines, *Faith Gabelnick, Jean MacGregor, Roberta S. Matthews, Barbara Leigh Smith*

TL40   Integrating Liberal Learning and Professional Education, *Robert A. Armour, Barbara S. Fuhrmann*

TL39   Teaching Assistant Training in the 1990s, *Jody D. Nyquist, Robert D. Abbott*

TL38   Promoting Inquiry in Undergraduate Learning, *Frederick Stirton Weaver*

TL37   The Department Chairperson's Role in Enhancing College Teaching, *Ann F. Lucas*

TL36   Strengthening Programs for Writing Across the Curriculum, *Susan H. McLeod*

TL35   Knowing and Doing: Learning Through Experience, *Pat Hutchings, Allen Wutzdorff*

TL34   Assessing Students' Learning, *Robert E. Young, Kenneth E. Eble*

TL33   College Teaching and Learning: Preparing for New Commitments, *Robert E. Young, Kenneth E. Eble*

TL32   Teaching Large Classes Well, *Maryellen Gleason Weimer*

TL31   Techniques for Evaluating and Improving Instruction, *Lawrence M. Aleamoni*

TL30   Developing Critical Thinking and Problem-Solving Abilities, *James E. Stice*

TL29   Coping with Faculty Stress, *Peter Seldin*

TL28   Distinguished Teachers on Effective Teaching, *Peter G. Beidler*